RICE.
NOODLES.
Yum.

RICE.
NOODLES.
Yum.

EVERYONE'S FAVORITE
SOUTHEAST ASIAN DISHES

ABIGAIL SOTTO RAINES

CREATOR OF MANILA SPOON

PAGE STREET
PUBLISHING CO.

PAGE STREET
PUBLISHING CO.

First published in 2019 by

Page Street Publishing Co.

27 Congress Street, Suite 105

Salem, MA 01970

www.pagestreetpublishing.com

Distributed by Macmillan, sales in Canada by The Canadian Manda Group.

23 22 21 20 19   1 2 3 4 5

ISBN-13: 978-1-62414-771-5

ISBN-10: 1-62414-771-2

Library of Congress Control Number: 2018957262

Cover and book design by Laura Gallant for Page Street Publishing Co.

Photography by Abigail Sotto Raines

Printed and bound in China

FOR MY FAMILY IN THE UNITED STATES

Mark, William and Sophie—for the unconditional love you all show me and for always being there when I need you. This book wouldn't be possible without you.

FOR MY FAMILY IN THE PHILIPPINES

Dad, Mom, Samuel and Eunice—for your continued support in anything I venture into and for inspiring me to be the best that I can be.

I love you all and I'm glad I have you all in my life, and this book is just my simple way of saying thank you!

CONTENTS

INTRODUCTION

Hi! I am Abby, a lawyer-turned-stay-at-home-mom, blogger and recipe developer at manilaspoon.com. If you've ever met any Filipinos, you'll know that our lives pretty much revolve around food. Our typical greetings often include, "Have you eaten already?" While others may talk about the weather, we always talk about food and what we've eaten or what we're about to eat! That's just the way it is.

Growing up on a tiny remote island, one of the 7,107 in the Philippine archipelago, my memories of childhood revolve around cooking and enjoying lots of good food. I was blessed to have my grandmother and mom, both amazing cooks, expose me to the delights of home cooking early on in life. Grandma lived with us for a while and when I was young she would often take me to the local market where she bought the ingredients for the family meal that day. On the weekends or sometimes after school I would help her make our *merienda* (snack) called saludsod— local pancakes made from arrowroot flour with fresh coconut filling. I still remember today just how delicious those pancakes were. Often we'd make a batch, turn our nipa hut (play area) into a store and sell them to neighbors and passersby on the street.

My mother was also a home economics teacher at the local school and was in charge of running the school canteen. I remember Friday nights spent helping her prepare overnight bread pudding casserole which we'd all have for breakfast the next day. We'd bake it in a makeshift homemade tin box heated by charcoal underneath (electricity was patchy in those days!). Yet, amazingly, the bread pudding always came out perfect. I truly admire my mom's ingenuity in making the best out of what we had.

Although Grandma and Mom were the best cooks I could ever emulate, when I grew up I initially didn't follow their footsteps. Instead, I became a lawyer like my father. I practiced law until I got married and moved with my husband to the United States. Little did I know that my love for food and passion for cooking would be rekindled after I got married. This was 15 years ago and I have been cooking and learning to cook each day since then. Occasionally, I still consult my mom on how to cook certain recipes, especially my favorite Filipino and Asian dishes.

So, why write a cookbook on rice and noodles? It's in my blood! In the Philippines, we eat rice at least three times a day—breakfast, lunch and dinner. This doesn't even count rice dishes as a snack or dessert! It is obviously a staple food in Southeast Asia and you won't believe the sheer number and deliciously creative ways of using rice. As for noodles, they are as much a part of the Southeast Asian diet as rice. Noodles can be eaten at every meal and are often incorporated as part of a celebration. In the Philippines no birthday or holiday season is complete without some version of pancit or our local noodle stir-fry on the table.

However, while millions of Southeast Asians eat rice and noodles every day, there's less exposure to these amazing foods on a worldwide scale. While there are some well-known rice and noodle dishes, they barely scratch the surface and there is so much more to discover beyond pad thai, pho and nasi goreng.

In this cookbook, I want to take you home to a typical Asian family and show you how they cook these delicious dishes made of rice and noodles. Having travelled extensively around Southeast Asia, I have come to learn about, appreciate and enjoy the rice and noodle dishes that each country has to offer. During the process, I have watched cooks show off their amazing talent in creating these mouth-watering dishes, what ingredients they used and when, where and how best to enjoy this food. This is what I attempt to bring to this cookbook—these delicious Asian rice and noodle dishes that you can easily make at home.

While it is true certain Asian dishes can have a lot of ingredients and may require some hands-on preparation like chopping and peeling ingredients here and there, the actual cooking itself is simple and for the most part you're done in a matter of minutes. The wonderful thing is since we have become so globalized, chances are there's an Asian grocery store in your neighborhood so ingredients that used to be hard to find are now readily available. I have tried to stay as close as possible to the authentic way of making these dishes including the original ingredients, but at the same time also providing substitutes whenever possible—but without sacrificing flavors and textures. The recipe notes will also provide shortcuts and tips to assist you in making these yummy dishes. Check out the Quick Guide to Ingredients and Helpful Tools for Asian Cooking on page 181 to learn more about the ingredients used in this cookbook.

Finally, remember that the key to making delicious Southeast Asian dishes is all about the balancing of flavors, contrasting yet complementary tastes of sweet, sour, salty, savory and spicy, or a combo of any of these, that come together harmoniously on a plate. With this in mind, you actually don't always need measurements; just let your taste buds be your guide. How do you achieve this? Taste. Taste. Taste. You'll see me repeating this throughout the cookbook. Taste the food as you cook and definitely toward the end of cooking the dish so you can adjust the flavors if you'd like.

So, if you've always wanted to make Asian rice and noodle dishes, this is the book for you. Let this be your guide but don't be scared to experiment and personalize the recipes to your liking. In no time, you can master your favorite Southeast Asian recipes from the comfort of your home!

I hope you enjoy all the dishes in this book as much as I have enjoyed creating them. Certainly, share the food you make from this book. After all, delicious food is best enjoyed with family and friends. Happy eating!

Mabuhay!

Abby

RICE 'N' EASY

I have heard this joke in the Philippines many times growing up: "You cannot get married until you know how to cook rice." This may seem funny or strange but knowing how to cook rice is so essential to Filipinos. Eating rice is just a part of who we are, not just in the Philippines but in the rest of Southeast Asia as well, so it really is of utmost importance for anyone who lives in this region to learn how to cook this staple food. We just can't survive without rice!

It is understandable that, for some, cooking rice can be intimidating. The rice may end up really mushy or still hard and uncooked in the middle or, worst of all, burnt underneath. But cooking rice need not be scary and this chapter will teach you how to make perfectly cooked rice—both regular (page 13) and sticky (page 33)—every time!

The best ingredient to use for making fried rice is cold cooked day-old rice, preferably the chilled leftovers you have in the fridge, so nothing is wasted. In this chapter, I give you the basics on how to make the easiest and tastiest Sinangag (Basic Garlic Fried Rice, page 14). You can make it plain or jazz it up with whatever meat or vegetables you have at hand.

The variety of fried rice dishes you can find around Southeast Asia is astounding. I have included the best and most popular rice dishes in the region that you can make from the comfort of your home. From the spicy Nasi Goreng Ayam (Fried Rice with Chicken, page 25) of Indonesia, to the slightly sweet and fruity Khao Pad Sapparot (Pineapple Fried Rice, page 17) from Thailand, the tasty yellow Java Rice (Yellow Fried Rice, page 21) from the Philippines and Com Chien Tom (Fried Rice with Prawn or Shrimp, page 26) from Vietnam, there's a rice dish to complement any meal.

Glutinous rice is a great substitute for regular boiled rice. For some fun rice side dishes, cubed Ketupat (Compressed Rice, page 22) or cone-shaped Balisungsong na Konin (Rice Cooked in Banana Leaves, page 29) are perfect to impress any guests. I have also included the national dish of Malaysia for good measure: Nasi Lemak (Rice Cooked in Coconut Milk, page 18). Nasi Lemak is made special by its accompanying garnishes, which turn this delicious rice into a meal on its own.

If you want a rice for special occasions, then Nasi Kuning (Festive Yellow Rice, page 30) is the perfect dish to try. This yellow rice from Indonesia is a very popular dish and is often served during festivities.

So, dive right in and make your first rice dish to enjoy with your family!

PERFECT RICE

Cooking rice shouldn't be a mystery. Whether you want to cook rice on the stovetop or in a rice cooker, this simple recipe and technique guarantees perfectly cooked rice every time. It's the foolproof way of making rice that will produce a perfectly fluffy and not mushy dish. I would recommend jasmine or basmati rice as these grains always hold their shape nicely when cooked, and they're quite fragrant, too.

SERVES 6 TO 8

2 cups (400 g) long-grain white rice like jasmine or basmati

3 cups (750 ml) water

NOTE: If using the measurement technique above, use the same cup for measuring the rice to measure the water. This ratio is always 1:1½— 1 cup (200 g) rice and 1½ cups (375 ml) water. This works best up to 2 cups (400 g) and perfectly with jasmine or basmati rice so use either for the best results.

Place the rice in a saucepan. Using your hands, rinse the rice with water twice, draining each time. After the second rinse, drain the rice in a fine strainer, shaking off any remaining water. Place the rice back into the saucepan and add the water. Bring to a boil over medium heat. When the water begins to boil, cover and adjust the heat to the lowest setting. Cook for 15 to 18 minutes, or until the water has been fully absorbed. Turn off the heat and let the rice sit undisturbed for another 10 minutes. Uncover, fluff the rice and serve immediately.

If you wish to cook more than 2 cups (400 g) of rice, or don't wish to measure at all, there's an easy and very reliable way to cook rice. The "finger technique," using your finger as a guide, is what's often used in Southeast Asia, where no measurement is done when cooking rice. With this guideline, you can cook as little or as much rice as you want.

Simply fill the saucepan with as much rice as you wish to cook. Rice expands to nearly three times its raw size so consider this when you add the rice to the pan. You don't want it to overflow. Rinse the rice twice as directed above and drain well. Return the rice to the pan and pat it down so it is level in the pan. Using one of your fingers measure the depth of the rice. Note where the top of the rice reaches your finger, using your thumb as marker. Place the same finger on top of the rice. Add enough water to reach the point that you marked with your thumb previously. Proceed to cook as above.

If you wish to make fried rice, use the finger technique, as the rice grains stay firm and hold their shape very well thus making it perfect for stir-frying. This is my tried and tested method for any fried rice dish I make and it works every time!

If you are using a rice cooker, either of the above measuring guides work. The only difference is that with the rice cooker you don't need to wait until the rice boils nor wait until it finishes cooking because the rice cooker does it all for you and automatically shuts off and shifts to the warm mode when the rice is cooked. Just leave the rice undisturbed for another 10 minutes when it's done then it's ready to be served.

SINANGAG
(Basic Garlic Fried Rice)

To say I love fried rice is an understatement. I love it so much that I cook a lot of rice just so I can have leftovers and make this fried rice. This garlicky-flavored rice is your basic foundation for any fried rice. Dress it up by adding your favorite meats and veggies to transform it into a full meal.

SERVES 4

2 tbsp (30 ml) cooking oil of choice

8 cloves garlic, minced

4 cups (645 g) cooked long-grain white rice like jasmine or basmati, cold or chilled

1 tsp salt, or to taste

3 stalks or about 2 tbsp (12 g) green onions, thinly sliced

Heat the cooking oil gently on a low setting in a wok or large frying pan. Add the minced garlic and cook until it's golden brown and crisp. Scoop out about 1 tablespoon (15 g) of the cooked garlic, drain on a paper towel and set aside.

Add the chilled rice to the pan and increase the heat to high. Press or pat down the rice using a spatula to separate the grains, then fold the rice over. Repeat these two steps a few times until the rice grains have fully separated. Season with the salt and cook for 3 to 5 minutes, or until the rice is fully heated through and fragrant. Transfer to a serving plate. Garnish with the reserved cooked garlic and green onions. Serve immediately.

NOTES: Another quick way to separate the rice grains before cooking is by using your fingers moistened with a little water. You can also simply sprinkle the rice with a little water. Work on the rice with your fingers until the grains are separated and no longer clumpy.

The key to making perfectly crisp garlic without burning it is to keep the heat on the lowest setting and simply allow the garlic to turn golden. It is worth the wait and by slowly cooking the garlic it imparts more flavor to the oil and certainly the rice, too.

KHAO PAD SAPPAROT
(Pineapple Fried Rice)

If you wish to impress your family and friends, this is the rice to make! This fancy fried rice combines the flavors of pineapples, raisins and nuts plus a hint of curry that work together to produce an exquisite array of tastes in your mouth. This dish can be made vegetarian, but it's common to add shrimp or chicken to the dish. Often served in a hollowed-out pineapple, it is sure to please the crowd every time!

SERVES 4

2 tbsp (30 ml) cooking oil of choice

12 oz (340 g) prawns or shrimps, peeled and deveined but with tails intact

4 cloves garlic, minced

1 onion, finely chopped

1 tbsp (15 g) curry powder, or more to taste

4 cups (645 g) cooked long-grain white rice like jasmine or basmati rice, cold or chilled

1 cup (150 g) raisins

1 cup (200 g) pineapple chunks (see Note)

½ cup (75 g) cashews

2 tomatoes, sliced and deseeded

2 tbsp (30 ml) fish sauce

1 tbsp (15 ml) oyster sauce

½ tbsp (8 g) sugar

Salt, to taste

3 stalks or about 2 tbsp (12 g) green onions, thinly sliced

Whole pineapple, for serving (optional)

In a wok or large skillet, heat the oil over medium-high. When the oil is hot, add the prawns and fry for 3 or 4 minutes or until fully cooked. Prawns are done when their flesh is fully opaque and bright pink. Scoop out the prawns, transfer to a plate and set aside.

Adjust the heat to medium-low. Add the garlic and onion to the pan and cook for 1 minute or until aromatic. Add the curry powder and cook briefly, stirring constantly, until fragrant.

Add the cooked rice to the pan and increase the heat to medium-high. Pat the rice grains down with a spatula, then fold the rice over. Do these two steps a few times until the rice grains have separated and the rice is fully coated with the curry powder. Add the raisins, pineapple, cashews and tomatoes and mix everything well. Return half of the cooked prawns to the wok. Season the mixture with the fish sauce, oyster sauce and sugar. Stir to mix well. Taste and adjust the seasoning with salt, if needed.

Transfer to a serving plate and garnish with the remaining prawns and green onions. You can also serve this inside a hollowed-out fresh pineapple, if you like.

NOTE: To serve this dish inside a pineapple, cut a pineapple in half lengthwise. Run a knife around the edges leaving at least ½ inch (13 mm) from the edge. Then, cut the pineapple flesh three to four times across and once down the center. Scoop out the pineapple chunks using a spoon and drain the remaining juice. Smooth out the bottom surface of the bowl. Cut the pineapple you sliced into chunks and use in making the fried rice. Place the fried rice inside the cut-up pineapple just before serving.

NASI LEMAK
(Rice Cooked in Coconut Milk)

This popular rice dish hails from Malaysia and is, in fact, its national dish. The rice is simmered in coconut milk and spices so it comes out flavorful. The accompaniments are what make this rice dish extra special—it's usually eaten with sambal, deep-fried anchovies, sliced cucumbers, fried peanuts and hard-boiled eggs, which makes it one deliciously satisfying meal!

SERVES 6

2 cups (400 g) long-grain white rice like jasmine or basmati

2 pandan leaves, cut or tied in a knot

1-inch (2.5-cm) piece ginger, peeled and sliced

1¾ cups (420 ml) water

1 cup (240 ml) coconut milk

1 tsp salt

Sambal or chili sauce, for serving

Hard-boiled eggs, for serving

Cucumber, sliced, for serving

Dried anchovies, deep-fried until light golden color, for serving

Fried peanuts, for serving

Rinse the rice twice. Drain well in a fine strainer. Place the rice, pandan leaves and sliced ginger in a pot. Add the water and bring to a boil. Adjust the heat to the lowest setting and cook covered for 15 to 18 minutes or until most of the water has been absorbed.

Mix the coconut milk with the salt. Pour this into the rice. Gently stir and then allow to simmer until the rice has dried up. Turn off the heat and let the rice sit undisturbed for another 10 minutes.

Alternatively, you can cook the rice in a rice cooker. Press the "Cook" button on the rice cooker to start cooking. Follow the rest of the instructions above. The rice cooker will automatically shut off and switch to warm mode when done.

Serve with sambal, hard-boiled eggs, cucumbers, anchovies and peanuts.

NOTE: Dried anchovies and bottled sambal or chili sauce may be purchased at any Asian store.

JAVA RICE
(Yellow Fried Rice)

Despite the "Java" in the name of this dish, this delicious rice is actually from the Philippines but perhaps had some Indonesian influence. With a bright deep-yellow color derived from turmeric, this tasty side dish lends a pop of color to any meal. It perfectly complements any barbecued or grilled meat, chicken or seafood. Chilled leftover rice is the best thing to use for this dish.

SERVES 4

2 tbsp (15 ml) cooking oil of choice

8 cloves garlic, minced

2 tbsp (30 g) butter

1 tsp ground turmeric

4 cups (645 g) cooked and chilled rice

1 tbsp (15 ml) soy sauce

½ tsp salt, or to taste

In a wok or large skillet, heat the oil and the garlic over low heat and cook until the garlic is nicely browned. Scoop out about 1 tablespoon (15 g) of the cooked garlic and set aside. Add the butter and ground turmeric to the pan and cook until the butter melts.

Add the rice to the pan and increase the heat to medium-high. Press or pat down the rice using a spatula to separate the grains, then fold the rice over. Do these two steps a few times until the rice grains have fully separated. Continue to cook until the rice is fully heated through and has turned yellowish in color. Make sure that the color is evenly distributed. Season the rice with the soy sauce and salt, stirring once more until the rice has fully absorbed the soy sauce. Taste and adjust the seasoning if needed. Serve immediately adding the remaining browned garlic as garnish.

KETUPAT
(Compressed Rice)

Ketupat are cubed rice cakes made from compressed rice. While traditionally this rice is cooked in a coconut leaf packet, nowadays it is cooked in a pot and then compressed. Ketupat is used as a side dish to both sweet and savory dishes. It is usually served with *kuah kacang* (peanut sauce), onions and cucumbers on the side.

SERVES 8

For the rice cakes

2 cups (400 g) uncooked broken rice or regular white rice such as jasmine

½ tsp salt

4 cups (1 L) water

For the kuah kacang (peanut sauce)

1 fresh or dried finger-length red chili

2 long red chilis or Fresno red peppers

3 cloves garlic, peeled and chopped

4 small shallots, chopped

3 stalks lemongrass, tough outer skin removed and using only the 3–4 inch (7.5–10 cm) white part at the bottom, chopped

1-inch (2.5-cm) piece galangal, peeled and chopped

2 tbsp (30 ml) cooking oil of choice

2 cups (250 g) roasted unsalted peanuts, coarsely ground

1 cup (240 ml) water

1 cup (240 ml) coconut milk

3 tbsp (30 ml) tamarind paste, or to taste

4 tbsp (30 g) sugar, or to taste

1 tsp salt, or to taste

Cucumbers, sliced, for serving (optional)

Onions, chopped, for serving (optional)

Rinse the rice well then drain. Place the rice and salt in a pot or rice cooker. Add the water and bring to a boil. Cover and adjust the heat to the lowest setting and cook the rice for 15 to 18 minutes or until the water has been fully absorbed. If using a rice cooker, simply press the "Cook" button and it will automatically cook the rice. Leave the rice undisturbed for another 10 minutes after the cooking cycle stops.

While the rice is cooking, prepare a square baking dish and line it with plastic wrap that comes up over the edges of the pan. Spoon the cooked rice into the dish and spread it evenly. Press down on the rice firmly, using a spatula. Cover with either wax paper or plastic wrap. Place a heavy weight on top of the rice. Leave it overnight or for at least several hours. When done, lift the rice out using the overhang from the plastic wrap. Cut the rice into cubes.

If using a dried red chili instead of fresh, soak in very hot water for about 15 minutes to rehydrate. Drain, then deseed all the chilis and chop. To make the peanut sauce, in a food processor or using a mortar and pestle, grind the chilis, garlic, shallots, lemongrass and galangal to a smooth paste.

Heat the oil over medium heat in a large pan. Add the chili paste and cook until aromatic. Add the peanuts. Pour in the water and coconut milk and allow the mixture to boil. Add the tamarind paste, sugar and salt. Bring down the heat to a simmer and cook until the sauce is thickened to your liking. Adjust the seasoning to your taste—it should be spicy, sweet and salty with a hint of subtle tartness.

Serve the ketupat with the peanut sauce and cucumbers and onions, if using. The peanut sauce is also great for satay and to serve atop cooked rice noodles!

NOTE: Galangal may be found fresh, dried or frozen in Asian stores. If you cannot find it, ginger may be used as substitute. The taste would be slightly different as the two ingredients have different flavor profiles.

NASI GORENG AYAM
(Fried Rice with Chicken)

This is the typical fried rice in Indonesia, with added flavors coming from fried shallots, chilis and sweet soy sauce. I love that with the addition of chicken or any meat you have at hand, this simple and tasty rice dish is transformed into a meal on its own.

SERVES 4

2 tbsp (30 ml) cooking oil of choice

4 medium shallots, sliced

3 stalks or about 2 tbsp (12 g) green onions, sliced diagonally

1 long red chili or red Fresno pepper, sliced diagonally

1½ cups (190 g) cooked chicken, chopped

1 tsp soy sauce, or to taste

4 cups (645 g) cooked cold or chilled white rice like jasmine or basmati

3 tbsp (45 ml) kecap manis or sweet soy sauce, or to taste

Salt and pepper, to taste

Fried egg, for garnish

Cucumber, sliced, for serving

Tomatoes, quartered, for serving

Heat the oil in a wok or large skillet over medium heat. Fry the shallots for about a minute. Add the green onions and sliced chili and mix well. Add the cooked chicken and season with the soy sauce. Add the rice, pressing down on the grains repeatedly until they separate. Fold the rice over a few times and cook until fully heated through. Add the kecap manis and stir to mix evenly. Taste and adjust seasoning with salt and pepper if desired. To serve, garnish with a fried egg on top along with sliced cucumbers and tomato wedges.

COM CHIEN TOM
(Fried Rice with Prawn or Shrimp)

It's amazing how many varieties of fried rice you can find in Southeast Asia. While there are similarities in each version, their flavors are unique and each have their own twist. Com Chien Tom is flavored with fish sauce and loaded with vegetables and prawns; this is a stand-out dish and you'll wish you always had extra rice on hand just so you can make this!

SERVES 3 TO 4

2 cups (320 g) leftover cooked cold white rice like jasmine or basmati

2 tbsp (30 ml) fish sauce

½ tsp ground turmeric (optional)

2 tbsp (30 ml) cooking oil of choice

6 cloves garlic, minced

10–12 large prawns or shrimps, peeled and deveined

2 eggs, lightly beaten

½ cup (75 g) French green beans, sliced into ¾-inch (2-cm) pieces

½ cup (55 g) carrots, julienned to roughly the same length as the green beans

1 oz (28 g) chopped fresh cilantro or coriander leaves, for garnish

1 red chili, sliced (optional)

Prepare the rice by sprinkling a little water on it to moisten and then separate the grains by rubbing them between your fingers. Set aside. Mix the fish sauce with the turmeric, if using, in a small bowl.

Heat the oil over medium heat in a wok or large skillet. Fry the garlic and prawns and cook until the prawns have turned opaque and bright pink. Push the prawns to one side of the wok. Pour the beaten eggs on the other side and allow them to set for a few seconds, then stir well. Mix the prawns and garlic with the eggs and cook briefly. Add the green beans and carrots and stir-fry for another minute. Add the prepared rice, increase the heat to high and cook for another 3 to 4 minutes or until the rice is fully heated through. Add the fish sauce mixture and then mix everything well until the rice is fully coated with the sauce. Garnish with fresh chopped cilantro and some fresh sliced chili, if desired.

Serve immediately.

NOTES: This dish cooks fast, so make sure all your ingredients are ready to go before cooking.

When choosing which fish sauce to buy, get the best and purest quality by choosing the one with the highest fish content and with little or no additives. It will make a huge difference in taste.

BALISUNGSONG NA KANIN
(Rice Cooked in Banana Leaves)

Balisungsong in Filipino means triangular or cone-shaped, hence the name adapted for these rice parcels cooked in cone-shaped banana leaves. Cooking rice in banana leaves adds fragrance and a subtle sweet flavor to the rice, so it's a very common method of cooking in Southeast Asia. Since the rice is cooked in individual parcels, it's also perfect for portion control.

SERVES 8 (16 PARCELS)

1½ cups (300 g) red rice

1½ cups (300 g) long-grain white rice like jasmine or basmati

16 banana leaf sheets cut into 6-inch (15-cm) lengths

5 cups (1.25 L) water

2 pandan leaves, tied in a knot

Rinse both types of rice well (at least twice) then drain and combine. Shape each banana leaf into a cone and fill with about ¼ cup (50 g) of the rice mixture. Fold over the top end to seal. Place the pointed side down in a saucepan or pot. Repeat until all the rice has been used. Pour the water into the saucepan or pot. Insert the pandan leaves into the pot. Place some more banana leaves on top, if you have extra.

Bring the mixture to a boil, then cover and simmer on low for 30 minutes or until the rice is done. Turn off the heat and remove the pot from the heat but leave the pot undisturbed for another 10 minutes. Using tongs, lift the cone parcels from the pot. Place the parcels on a plate and peel off the banana leaves before eating.

NASI KUNING

(Festive Yellow Rice)

This iconic cone-shaped yellow rice is cooked with coconut milk and turmeric, which gives the rice its yellowish glow. This dish is very popular on the islands of Indonesia and is always served on special occasions. It is pleasant in taste, has a tender texture, and is also quite fragrant thanks to the addition of kaffir lime leaves.

SERVES 6

1 cup (200 g) long-grain white rice like jasmine or basmati

1 cup (200 g) sticky or glutinous white rice

1 (13.5-oz [400-ml]) can coconut milk

1½ cups (360 ml) water

2 tsp (10 g) ground turmeric

¾ tsp salt

5 kaffir lime leaves

Cucumbers, sliced, for serving (optional)

Tomatoes, chopped, for serving (optional)

Prawn crackers, for serving (optional)

Fried peanuts, for serving (optional)

Fried anchovies, for serving (optional)

Rinse the long-grain rice and sticky rice twice. Drain well. Place the rice in a pot. Combine the coconut milk and water, then stir in the ground turmeric and salt. Add the coconut milk mixture to the pot with the rice. Add the kaffir lime leaves and bring the mixture to a boil over medium heat then adjust the heat to low, cover and cook for 20 to 25 minutes or until the liquid has been fully absorbed by the rice. Turn off the heat and leave the rice undisturbed for another 10 minutes. Alternatively, you can also cook this in a rice cooker. Serve immediately with the cucumbers, tomatoes, prawn crackers, fried peanuts and fried anchovies on the side, if desired.

NOTES: Kaffir lime leaves are available fresh or frozen at any Asian store. If you cannot find them, simply replace them with some lemon peel.

Use a plastic funnel to form the cone-shaped rice. Mold the rice into the funnel while it is still hot.

PERFECT STEAMED STICKY OR GLUTINOUS RICE

We love steamed sticky rice in Southeast Asia. It's unbelievable how many dishes can be created out of this delicious gluey rice. You don't need a lot of add-ins to enjoy this—it's delicious on its own and can accompany pretty much any dish that calls for regular rice. So, if the usual boiled rice becomes boring, then save the day with this perfectly steamed glutinous rice!

SERVES 4

3 cups (600 g) sticky or glutinous white rice

Banana leaves or cheesecloth (big enough to fit in your steamer)

2 pandan leaves tied in a knot (optional)

Place the rice in a bowl and cover with water to about 2 inches (5 cm) above the rice. Soak the rice overnight or for at least 3 hours.

Rinse the rice twice or until the water runs clear. Drain. Line a steamer tray or basket with banana leaves or a cheesecloth if the holes won't hold the rice grains. Place the rice on top then add the pandan leaves, if using.

In a saucepan or wok, add enough water for steaming. Bring the water to a rolling boil. Place the steamer tray or basket in the wok or on top of a saucepan ensuring that the water doesn't touch the food. Cover and steam for 30 minutes over rapidly boiling water or until the rice is tender but still retaining some chewiness. Remove the wok from the heat and allow it to sit undisturbed for about 5 minutes. Transfer the rice to a serving plate and eat immediately.

NOTE: If not using right away, store the cooked rice in an airtight container so it doesn't dry up. It's best to consume the rice on the same day it is cooked, as it will dry out over time.

DELICIOUS NOODLE DISHES

There are so many varieties of delicious noodle recipes from Southeast Asia that I honestly found it hard to limit the recipes I wanted to include in this chapter. For a while, I couldn't make up my mind up but kept on adding to the list and re-arranging them every so often. I wanted to have a broad representation of the kinds of noodles and range of flavors you can find in the region, so this chapter is not limited to just a few stir-fries.

Naturally, the classic noodle dishes that are familiar to many are here. Of course I include the ever-popular Pad Thai (page 50) with its sweet, sour, salty flavors with an optional spicy kick. Mee Goreng Mamak (Yellow Noodles in Sweet and Spicy Sauce, page 49) is a flavorful pan-fried noodle dish spiced with chili paste commonly sold on the streets of Malaysia, Indonesia and Singapore. Pancit Bihon Guisado (Filipino Noodle Stir-Fry, page 38) is the Philippines' favorite birthday and celebration noodle dish, seasoned with soy sauce and oyster sauce and often cooked with chicken, pork or shrimp and always with cabbage and carrots.

Have you ever tried dishes with flat and really wide rice noodles? If not, you're in for a treat! These noodles are called "ho fun" in Chinese and may be found fresh or frozen in Asian stores and are quite popular in Southeast Asia. My two favorite dishes that use these flat noodles are Char Kway Teow (Stir-Fried Flat Rice Noodles, page 53), a big hawker favorite in Malaysia and Singapore; and the unforgettable Pad See Ew (Flat Noodles Stir-Fried in Soy Sauce, page 57) from Thailand.

Vietnam is famous for its fresh noodle bowls so it is perfectly appropriate to include Bun Tom Xao (Stir-Fried Lemongrass Prawns with Rice Noodles, page 46) to the mix; it is made with prawns or shrimp stir-fried in lemongrass and ginger-flavored sauce then placed on top of rice noodles and eaten with fresh herbs and greens on the side.

Wait! There's so much more, including Mee Kati (Rice Vermicelli in Coconut Milk, page 54), Mee Grob (Crispy Noodles in Sweet and Sour Sauce, page 41) and Hokkien Mee (Thick Yellow Noodles Cooked in Black Sauce, page 37). If you are looking for a tasty and meaty sauce over noodles then the Guay Tiew Neua Sap (Rice Noodles with Curried Beef Gravy, page 42) is for you! Mildly spiced with curry powder, this yummy dish is perfect for the entire family.

I saved the best for last: the inimitable Pancit Palabok (Rice Noodles in Shrimp Sauce, page 45), because it is uniquely Filipino. There are many variations of this dish, but the common theme is the shrimp-based sauce made from scratch with a bright yellow-orange color. The delicious sauce is smothered over rice vermicelli then garnished with green onions, flaked smoked fish and crushed pork crackling. It makes a beautiful presentation on a plate and is surely a crowd-pleasing dish.

A variety of seasonings and different kinds of soy sauce are used in these delectable noodle treats. Check out my quick guide on ingredients for Southeast Asian cooking on page 181 to learn more about these seasonings that truly elevate these dishes to the top!

Which one would you like to try first?

HOKKIEN MEE
(Thick Yellow Noodles Cooked in Black Sauce)

The use of dark soy sauce gives this tasty noodle dish an eye-catching hue. With prawn or shrimp and chicken and pork belly added to the mix, you're sure to enjoy this very tasty Malaysian staple. It's also simple to make and one that you'll add to your menu rotation.

SERVES 6

1 (1-lb [455-g]) package cooked hokkien mee or udon noodles

3 tbsp (45 ml) dark soy sauce

1 tbsp (15 ml) light (regular) soy sauce

1 tbsp (15 ml) oyster sauce

1½ tbsp (23 g) palm sugar or brown sugar

2 tsp (10 g) cornstarch

1 cup (240 ml) water

1 tbsp (15 ml) cooking oil of choice

5 oz (150 g) pork belly, thinly sliced

6 cloves garlic, minced

8 oz (225 g) chicken breast or boneless thighs, halved then sliced very thinly

8 oz (225 g) prawns or shrimps, peeled and deveined

8 stalks of gai lan (Chinese broccoli) or broccoli rabe, thick bottom stalk cut off with leaves and thin stalks sliced to about 2 inches (5 cm) long

2 cups (105 g) Chinese or napa cabbage, chopped

2 limes, sliced, for serving

Rinse the hokkien mee or udon noodles in cold water to refresh; drain, then set aside.

Combine the dark soy sauce, light soy sauce, oyster sauce and sugar in a bowl, then set aside. In another bowl, stir the cornstarch into the water. Set aside.

Heat the oil in a wok or large skillet over medium heat. Fry the pork belly until it is nicely browned and crispy. Add the garlic and let sizzle for 30 seconds or until aromatic. Add the chicken and fry for 2 minutes or until the chicken has turned white. Add the prawns and continue to cook for another minute. Add the noodles, the soy sauce mixture and the slurry and cook for 2 to 3 minutes. Add the gai lan and cabbage and continue to cook for another 1 to 2 minutes or until the veggies are tender but not mushy. Transfer to a serving plate and serve with limes on the side.

NOTES:
Udon and hokkien mee noodles are available for purchase at any Asian grocery. You may find them in the refrigerated section of the store. If you cannot find cooked hokkien mee or udon, just replace with fresh (but uncooked) noodles. Follow the package directions on how to cook them.

Light soy sauce is not reduced sodium-soy sauce. It is the regular soy sauce used for both dipping and cooking. It is called light because it is thinner in consistency and to differentiate it from the dark and thicker dark soy sauce, which has less salt and is used primarily for color. To learn more about the various types of soy sauces used in this book, see page 183.

PANCIT BIHON GUISADO
(Filipino Noodle Stir-Fry with Meat and Vegetables)

No celebration is complete without pancit! Whether it is a birthday, wedding, anniversary, Christmas or any holiday, this dish will always be on every Filipino table. It is our ultimate comfort food—noodles cooked in soy sauce with lots of vegetables and your choice of meat and served with some freshly squeezed lime for that added citrus goodness!

SERVES 8 TO 10

1 lb (455 g) dried pancit bihon rice sticks or rice vermicelli

2 tbsp (30 ml) cooking oil of choice

8 oz (225 g) prawns or shrimps

4 cloves garlic, peeled and minced

1 medium onion, peeled and chopped

3 Chinese sausages, soaked in hot water for 5 minutes, sliced diagonally

8 oz (225 g) chicken breast, thinly sliced

2 cups (110 g) carrots, julienned

2 cups (200 g) green beans, thinly sliced diagonally

2 cups (100 g) Napa or Savoy cabbage, coarsely chopped

Salt and pepper, to taste

2 cups (480 ml) water

½ cup (120 ml) soy sauce

2 tbsp (30 ml) oyster sauce

2 tsp (10 g) sugar

Fresh limes, sliced, for serving

Place the rice noodles in a pan filled with room-temperature water and soak for about 30 minutes or until softened. Drain well, then trim into shorter lengths with scissors for easier handling. Set aside.

Heat the oil in a big wok or large skillet over medium-high heat. Fry the prawns for 3 to 4 minutes or until they are fully opaque and bright pink. Transfer them to a plate and set aside. In the same pan, fry the garlic and onion for 1 minute or until very aromatic. Add the Chinese sausage and chicken and cook for another 2 minutes. Add the carrots, green beans and cabbage and stir-fry for another 2 minutes or just until the vegetables are tender-crisp. Season lightly with a little salt and pepper, to taste. Remove about half of the contents of the wok and set aside. Keep warm.

Pour the water into the wok. Add the soy sauce, oyster sauce and sugar. Bring to a boil, then simmer on low for 1 to 2 minutes. Add the drained rice noodles and half of the cooked prawns. Stir everything to ensure that the noodles get soaked in the sauce. Cook, stirring often, until the noodles are soft and the sauce has been fully absorbed. Taste and adjust the seasoning with a little soy sauce or salt and pepper if needed. Transfer to a plate and top with the remaining vegetables and chicken mixture and the reserved prawns.

Serve immediately with some slices of lime on the side. Squeeze a few drops of fresh lime juice on the noodles before eating for that extra tang!

NOTE: Pancit bihon can be found in the noodle section of many Asian stores. Use noodles imported from the Philippines to make a truly authentic pancit and because they work best for this recipe.

MEE GROB
(Crispy Noodles in Sweet and Sour Sauce)

Sweet, sour, crunchy and with a hint of citrus, this crispy fried noodle dish makes a delicious snack or light lunch with all the right textures and flavors. It is so good, it is destined to become a household favorite!

SERVES 4

2 cups (480 ml) cooking oil of choice or more as needed, for frying

4 oz (115 g) dried rice vermicelli

3 cloves garlic, minced

1 shallot, finely chopped

12 oz (340 g) raw prawns or shrimps, peeled and deveined

7 oz (200 g) puffed or fried tofu

2 tbsp (30 ml) tamarind paste

2 tbsp (25 g) sugar

2 tbsp (30 ml) fish sauce

1 tbsp (15 ml) lime juice

6 kaffir lime leaves, finely shredded

3 stalks or about 2 tbsp (12 g) green onions, thinly sliced, for serving

1 cup (60 g) bean sprouts, for serving

2 finger-length red chilis, sliced, for serving

Heat the oil in a saucepan to medium or about 350°F (175°C). The oil is hot enough when bubbles form at the edge of a wooden skewer dipped into the oil. Break the noodles into pieces. Drop the noodles, a small portion at a time, into the oil. Cook just until they puff up, in about 2 to 3 seconds, and then scoop them out with a strainer and place them in a bowl lined with paper towels to drain excess oil. Place the fried noodles on a platter and set aside.

Measure about 1 tablespoon (15 ml) from the oil used for frying then heat it in a wok over medium heat. Fry the garlic and shallot for 1 minute. Add the prawns and fried tofu and cook for 3 to 4 minutes or until the prawns change color and have turned fully opaque. Add the tamarind paste, sugar, fish sauce, lime juice and kaffir lime leaves. Toss all the ingredients together briefly. Remove the pan from the heat.

Top the cooked noodles with the prawn mixture. Garnish with green onions, bean sprouts and sliced chilis. Mix everything quickly and serve immediately so the fried noodles will retain their crunch.

GUAY TIEW NEUA SAP

(Rice Noodles with Curried Beef Gravy)

I feel like this is the Asian version of the Italian classic spaghetti Bolognese. The two dishes don't taste the same, obviously, but they are equally delicious! This Thai version is perfectly spiced, so filling and satisfying that you don't need any other dishes to go with it. It is full comfort food on its own!

SERVES 6

4 tbsp (60 ml) cooking oil of choice, divided

3 cloves garlic, minced

1 small onion, finely chopped

1 tbsp (15 g) yellow curry powder, or to taste

1 lb (455 g) ground beef

1 tbsp (15 ml) fish sauce

2 tsp (10 g) sugar

½ tsp freshly ground black pepper

1 cup (240 ml) beef stock

2 plum tomatoes, diced

1 tsp cornstarch

2 tbsp (30 ml) soy sauce

Salt and pepper, to taste

1 lb (455 g) dried guay tiew (flat rice noodles), soaked in room-temperature water for 1 hour or until softened

¼ cup (60 ml) sweet soy sauce

1 small head of lettuce, leaves separated

1 oz (28 g) fresh cilantro, chopped, for serving

Heat 2 tablespoons (30 ml) of the oil over medium heat in a large skillet or frying pan. Fry the garlic and onion for about 1 minute or until very aromatic. Add the curry powder and fry briefly just until fragrant. Add the ground beef, fish sauce, sugar and black pepper. Cook, stirring frequently, until the beef becomes crumbly and has fully browned.

Pour the stock in the cooked beef and add the tomatoes. Simmer over low for 15 minutes. Combine the cornstarch with the soy sauce in a small bowl then add to the beef mixture, stir well and cook just until the sauce has thickened slightly. Taste and adjust the seasoning with a bit of salt and pepper if desired. Keep warm.

Place the softened rice noodles in a large bowl. Drizzle the sweet soy sauce all over the noodles and mix until the noodles are coated in the sauce. In a wok or skillet, preferably nonstick, heat the remaining 2 tablespoons (30 ml) of oil over medium-heat. Stir-fry the noodles for 3 to 5 minutes or until soft but not mushy. Remove the noodles from the wok.

To serve, place some lettuce leaves on a large platter or individual bowls. Add the noodles then spoon the cooked beef on top. Garnish with some chopped cilantro.

PANCIT PALABOK
(Rice Noodles in Shrimp Sauce)

All Philippine noodles are called pancit but for me, this is the ultimate pancit recipe as it's so uniquely Filipino. With a delicious homemade shrimp sauce and topped with eggs, pork cracklings, smoked fish and herbs your taste buds are in for a yummy treat!

SERVES 8

8 oz (225 g) dried palabok noodles or rice vermicelli (pancit bihon)

4 tbsp (60 g) dried large shrimp

4¼ cups (1 L) water, divided

2 tbsp (15 g) annatto seeds

1 lb (455 g) raw prawns or shrimps, peeled and deveined, reserving the heads

2 tbsp (30 ml) cooking oil of choice, divided

2 shallots, chopped

3 cloves garlic, minced

8 oz (225 g) ground pork

2 tbsp (30 ml) fish sauce

1 tbsp (15 g) sugar

3 tbsp (45 g) cornstarch diluted in 1 tbsp (15 ml) water

2 tsp (10 g) smoked paprika

3 cups (180 g) Napa cabbage, shredded or coarsely chopped

Salt and pepper, to taste

½–1 cup (58–115 g) flaked smoked fish, to taste

Crushed chicharon or pork cracklings

Green onions, sliced thinly

Hard-boiled eggs, halved

Crushed peanuts

Calamansi or limes, sliced

Cook the palabok noodles according to package directions. If using rice vermicelli or rice sticks (pancit bihon), cook in boiling water for 3 to 4 minutes or until soft. Rinse with cold water then drain and set aside.

Rehydrate the dried shrimp in 3 cups (720 ml) of hot water for 10 minutes or until plump. Drain the shrimp and reserve the liquid. Meanwhile, soak the annatto seeds in ¼ cup (60 ml) of very hot, freshly boiled water for 10 to 15 minutes, squeezing the seeds to release their color. Set aside.

Cook half of the peeled raw prawns in very hot water until they turn opaque and bright pink. Set aside for garnish. Chop the remaining half of the prawns for cooking.

In a saucepan, heat 1 tablespoon (15 ml) of the oil over medium heat and fry the prawn heads until they turn pink. Add the rehydrated shrimp to the pan and cook for another minute. Add the reserved 3 cups (750 ml) of shrimp water plus an additional 1 cup (240 ml) water. Simmer the stock for 10 minutes and strain well, reserving the broth. Discard the shrimp and set aside the broth.

In a saucepan, heat the remaining tablespoon (15 ml) of oil over medium heat and fry the shallots and garlic for a minute or until aromatic. Add the ground pork and cook until browned all over. Season with the fish sauce and sugar. Add the raw chopped prawns and give it a quick stir. Pour in the shrimp broth and strain the liquid from the annatto seeds over the mixture, discarding the seeds, then simmer for 3 to 5 minutes. Add the cornstarch diluted in water and the smoked paprika and cook, stirring. Add the shredded Napa cabbage and cook for 1 minute or until it's tender but not mushy. Adjust seasoning with salt and pepper if desired.

To serve, place a portion of the noodles on a plate and top with the sauce. Garnish with the reserved cooked shrimp, flaked smoked fish, crushed chicharon, green onions, hard-boiled eggs and crushed peanuts. Squeeze a few drops of lime juice over the dish before eating.

BUN TOM XAO
(Stir-Fried Lemongrass Prawn with Rice Noodles)

The dressing alone gives a lot of flavor to this Vietnamese noodle bowl dish. But the star of the plate is the prawns sautéed in ginger and lemongrass sauce with a spicy kick from the chili. Placed on top of noodles with some fresh herbs and greens, the entire dish is sure to impress anyone!

SERVES 4

2 tbsp (30 ml) fish sauce

3 tbsp (45 g) sugar, divided

2 tbsp (30 ml) lime juice

2 tbsp (30 ml) water

5 cloves garlic, minced, divided

1 finger-length red chili, sliced

8 oz (225 g) dried rice vermicelli

1 tbsp (15 ml) cooking oil of choice

1 tbsp (15 g) freshly grated ginger

2 tbsp (30 g) lemongrass, tough outer skin removed and using only the 3–4 inch (7.5–10 cm) bottom white part, finely chopped

1 long red chili, seeded and sliced (optional)

1 onion, chopped

12 oz (340 g) prawns or shrimps, peeled and deveined

1½ tbsp (23 ml) fish sauce

1½ tbsp (23 ml) oyster sauce

1 small head of lettuce, torn

¼ cup (13 g) basil leaves, chopped

¼ cup (13 g) mint, chopped

¼ cup (13 g) cilantro or coriander leaves, chopped

1 cup (110 g) cucumber, julienned

1 cup (110 g) carrots, julienned or shredded

Roasted peanuts, crushed, for serving

Fried shallots, for serving

Mix the fish sauce, 2 tablespoons (30 g) of sugar, lime juice and water in a bowl until the sugar is fully dissolved. Add 2 cloves minced garlic and finger-length chili. Set aside.

Cook the rice noodles in boiling water for 3 to 4 minutes or until soft. Drain and rinse with cold water. Set aside.

Heat the oil in a wok or large skillet over medium heat. Add the remaining garlic, ginger, lemongrass and long-red chili, if using, and cook for 30 seconds or until fragrant. Increase the heat to high, add the onion and cook for 1 minute. Add the prawns with the fish sauce, oyster sauce and 1 tablespoon (15 g) of sugar and stir-fry for 3 to 4 minutes or until the prawns are opaque and bright pink. Remove from heat.

To serve, place some lettuce at the bottom of four bowls. Divide the noodles into each bowl. Top the noodles with any or all of the following: basil, mint, cilantro, cucumber and carrots. Then top with the cooked prawns.

Garnish with the crushed peanuts and fried shallots. Serve with the fish sauce on the side.

MEE GORENG MAMAK
(Yellow Noodles in Sweet and Spicy Sauce)

When I visited Kuala Lumpur last summer, I asked a local what dish she would recommend that I try first. Without hesitation she said, "mamak." "You can find it everywhere," she continued, "and it's so delicious." She was right indeed! Sweet, spicy, savory and so flavorful, this noodle dish will blow your taste buds away!

SERVES 4

8 oz (225 g) dried egg noodles (like pancit canton) or 1 lb (455 g) fresh egg noodles (like lo mein)

2 tbsp (30 ml) dark soy sauce

3 tbsp (45 ml) sweet soy sauce

3 tbsp (45 ml) ketchup

1 tbsp (15 g) brown sugar

3 tbsp (45 ml) cooking oil of choice, divided

3 cloves garlic, minced

1 shallot, finely chopped

8 oz (225 g) chicken breast, halved then thinly sliced

½ cup (100 g) pressed or fried tofu, cubed

1 tbsp (15 g) sambal or chili paste (see Note)

1 long hot green chili, sliced diagonally

2 eggs, beaten

2 cups (120 g) choy sum or small mustard greens, about 8–10 pieces, chopped (leaving out the tough ends)

2 cups (106 g) bean sprouts

Salt and pepper, to taste

This dish takes just a few minutes to cook, so make sure everything is ready before you start cooking.

If using dried noodles, cook for 3 to 4 minutes in boiling water. Rinse with cold water then drain. Set aside. If using fresh noodles, quickly blanch in boiling water for 45 seconds, stirring to separate the strands. Drain then immediately rinse with cold water. With fresh noodles, it's best to blanch them just before cooking so the noodles don't stick together.

To make the seasoning sauce, combine the dark soy sauce, sweet soy sauce, ketchup and brown sugar. Set aside.

In a wok or large skillet, heat 2 tablespoons (30 ml) of the oil over medium-high heat, then add the garlic and shallot. Stir-fry for about 1 minute or until aromatic. Add the chicken and cook until it turns white. Add the tofu, sambal and the chopped green chili and cook for another minute. Push the ingredients to one side. Add the remaining tablespoon (15 ml) of oil to the pan and then add the beaten eggs. Allow the eggs to set for a few seconds then scramble. Add the noodles and the seasoning sauce and toss the ingredients, cooking for 2 to 3 minutes or until the noodles are tender and fully coated with the sauce. Stir in the choy sum and the bean sprouts and cook briefly, less than a minute, just until they are beginning to wilt but still retaining some crispness. Taste and adjust the seasoning with salt and pepper if desired. It should be spicy, sweet and savory. Transfer to a plate and serve immediately.

NOTE: You can make your own chili paste by simply rehydrating dried red chilis for 15 minutes in hot water. You can enhance the sauce with some minced shallots, a little sugar and some dried shrimp paste for extra flavor. For convenience, you can also buy bottled sambal at any Asian store.

PAD THAI
(Stir-Fried Rice Noodles)

Cooking Pad Thai is a bit tricky because it cooks so fast over high heat. Thankfully, it's not impossible to make a tasty version at home that can rival a restaurant-made dish. The key is to have everything ready before you cook and to cook in small batches—this will enable you to cook the noodles perfectly without the dish turning into a gooey mess. I know this based on experience and through knowledge gained by attending cooking classes in Thailand.

SERVES 3 TO 4

6 oz (170 g) dried Thai rice noodles (medium to large size)

4 tbsp (45 g) white sugar, plus more for garnish

3 tbsp (45 ml) tamarind paste or sauce (see Note)

2 tbsp (30 ml) rice vinegar

2 tbsp (30 ml) fish sauce

1 tsp hot chili sauce (like Sriracha), optional

½ tsp chili powder (optional)

2 tbsp (30 ml) cooking oil of choice, divided

3 cloves garlic, minced

1 shallot, finely chopped

1 tbsp (15 g) large dried shrimp

12–14 raw large prawns or shrimps, peeled and deveined

½ cup (100 g) pressed or fried tofu, cubed

2 tbsp (30 g) pickled white radish, minced

2 eggs

1 cup (60 g) bean sprouts, plus extra for topping

½ cup (24 g) Chinese chives or about 4–6 stalks, sliced into 1-inch (2.5-cm) lengths, plus a few extra for garnish

4 tbsp (60 g) coarsely ground peanuts, plus more for garnish

Limes, quartered, for garnish

Chili flakes, for garnish

Soak the dried noodles in room temperature water for 30 to 45 minutes, or until soft. The noodles are soft when you can wrap a strand around your finger. Drain and set aside.

To make the seasoning sauce, combine the sugar, tamarind paste, rice vinegar, fish sauce, hot chili sauce and chili powder, if using. Mix well and set aside.

Heat 1 tablespoon (15 ml) of the oil over medium-high heat then fry the garlic and shallot until aromatic. Increase the heat to high then add the dried shrimp, raw prawns and tofu and cook for about 1 minute. Add the noodles and cook for 2 to 3 minutes or until tender. Stir the noodles in a circular motion using the corner edge of a spatula. This will ensure the noodles won't tear. Add the pickled radish and the seasoning sauce and toss the mixture to absorb the sauce. Cook for another minute or until the mixture is nearly dry.

Push all the ingredients to one side, add the remaining oil and crack the eggs in. Allow the eggs to set briefly for a few seconds, then scramble and mix with the noodles. Add the bean sprouts, chives and chopped peanuts. Fold quickly to mix everything. Transfer to a plate and serve immediately with a lime wedge, extra crushed nuts, chili flakes and a little sugar on the side.

NOTE: Tamarind paste or sauce may be purchased at any Asian store or online. Brands vary in taste in terms of intensity and concentration and some may be darker in color than others, so this may affect how much you need to use for your Pad Thai sauce. If using the darker tamarind concentrate, use about 2 tablespoons (30 ml) and omit the rice vinegar. Taste the sauce and adjust the amount according to your preference. The Pad Thai sauce should be a good balance of sour, sweet and salty with a little spicy kick if you like.

CHAR KWAY TEOW
(Malaysian Stir-Fried Flat Rice Noodles)

You will find this stir-fried noodle dish all over Malaysia and Singapore and for good reason—it's so flavorful with just the right amount of spicy kick and savory goodness coming from a combination of two kinds of soy sauces. Add some prawns and fish cakes to the mix and you have one fabulous meal!

SERVES 4

1 tbsp (15 ml) light (regular) soy sauce

1 tbsp (15 ml) dark soy sauce

1 tbsp (15 ml) oyster sauce

1 tbsp (15 g) sugar

1 tbsp (15 ml) water

10 oz (300 g) fresh flat and wide rice noodles (ho fun)

2 tbsp (30 ml) cooking oil of choice, divided

3 cloves garlic, peeled and chopped

8 oz (225 g) prawns or shrimps, peeled and deveined or chicken breasts, thinly sliced

1 tbsp (15 g) sambal or chili paste

1 cup (100 g) fish cakes or fish tofu, thinly sliced (see Note)

2 eggs

1 cup (60 g) bean sprouts

½ cup (35 g) Chinese chives, or 4–6 stalks, cut into 1-inch (2.5-cm) lengths, plus more for garnish

Salt and pepper, to taste

This noodle dish cooks very quickly, so everything must be ready and at hand once you start to cook.

Combine the light soy sauce, dark soy sauce, oyster sauce, sugar and water in a bowl. Pour half of the sauce onto the noodles and stir to coat. Set aside the rest.

Heat 1 tablespoon (15 ml) of the oil in a nonstick wok or large skillet over medium heat. Stir-fry the garlic until it is fragrant and starting to brown. Increase the heat to high, then add the prawns and cook for 1 minute. If using chicken instead, cook the chicken for a couple of minutes or until it has turned white. Stir in the sambal and fish cakes and cook for another minute.

Add the noodles and toss for 1 minute. Pour in the remaining sauce then continue to toss the noodles for another 1 to 2 minutes or until soft.

Push the noodles to one side to create a space in the wok. Add the remaining 1 tablespoon (15 ml) of oil and the eggs. Quickly scramble the eggs then combine with the noodles. Add the bean sprouts and chopped chives and stir to mix all the ingredients and cook just until the vegetables are beginning to wilt. Taste and adjust the seasoning with salt and pepper, if desired. Remove from the heat. Serve hot.

NOTE: Fish cakes are available in Asian stores. If unavailable, frozen fish tofu may be used instead. Just thaw before using.

MEE KATI
(Rice Vermicelli in Coconut Milk)

My husband totally fell in love with this dish when I made it for him. And why not? Rice noodles are steeped in a perfectly seasoned and creamy coconut milk sauce and soak up the sweet, sour, salty and savory flavors of the sauce. It is so good! Serve with extra red chilis on the side for some spicy kick!

SERVES 4 TO 6

8 oz (225 g) dried rice vermicelli

3 tbsp (45 ml) cooking oil of choice, divided

2 eggs, beaten

8 oz (225 g) prawns or shrimps, shelled, deveined but with tails on

1 medium onion, peeled and chopped

1 (13.5-oz [400-ml]) can coconut milk

¼ cup (60 g) salted soybeans, smashed (measured after smashing)

2 tbsp (30 g) sugar

2 tbsp (30 g) tamarind paste

3 stalks or about 2 tbsp (12 g) green onions, thinly sliced

2 cups (120 g) bean sprouts

Fresh cilantro, chopped, for serving

Red chilis, sliced, for serving

Limes, quartered, for serving

Soak the noodles in room-temperature water for 30 minutes or until soft. Drain and trim into shorter lengths. Set aside.

Heat 1 tablespoon (15 ml) of the oil in a frying pan or skillet over medium heat and add the eggs, tilting the pan to spread the eggs all over and form an omelet. Cook until the eggs are set, then flip and cook for another minute or until done. Remove the egg to a flat surface, roll it up, then slice it into thin strips. Set aside.

Add 1 tablespoon (15 ml) of oil to a wok or large skillet over medium-high heat. Fry the prawns for 3 to 4 minutes or until fully opaque and bright pink. Remove the prawns from the pan and set aside.

Add the remaining tablespoon (15 ml) of oil to the wok and stir-fry the onion for 2 minutes or until very fragrant and beginning to turn light brown in color. Pour in the coconut milk with the salted soybeans, sugar and tamarind paste. Bring to a boil, then lower the heat and simmer for 5 minutes.

Add the soaked rice noodles, coat them with the sauce and cook until most of the sauce has been absorbed. Return half of the prawns to the wok with the green onions and bean sprouts and cook for another minute.

Transfer the cooked noodles to a platter or individual plates and garnish with the remaining prawns, cilantro, chilis and lime slices.

PAD SEE EW

(Flat Noodles Stir-Fried in Soy Sauce)

Pad See Ew is a very popular Thai street food right up there with Pad Thai! It's easy to make and comes together so quickly. A sweet-salty sauce that's all soaked up by the fresh noodles and then caramelized in the wok makes this a sure winner!

SERVES 4

2 tbsp (30 ml) dark soy sauce

1 tbsp (15 ml) fish sauce

1 tbsp (15 ml) oyster sauce

2½ tbsp (38 g) sugar

8 oz (225 g) chicken breast, halved lengthwise and then thinly sliced

1 tbsp (15 ml) soy sauce

10 oz (300 g) flat and wide fresh rice noodles (ho fun, see Note)

4 tbsp (60 ml) cooking oil of choice, divided

3 cloves garlic, minced

1 egg, beaten

8 stalks of gai lan (Chinese broccoli) or broccoli rabe, thick bottom stalk cut off, with leaves and thin stalks sliced to about 2 inches (5 cm) long

Freshly ground black pepper, to taste

NOTE: Fresh wide rice noodles (ho fun) are great for this dish. You can find these flat rice noodles at Asian stores either in the refrigerated or frozen section. If frozen, thaw first before using. If you cannot find fresh or frozen noodles, simply use extra-large dried Thai rice noodles available in Asian stores and soak them in room temperature water for about an hour or until softened.

This noodle dish cooks very quickly, so everything must be ready and at hand once you start to cook.

To make the seasoning sauce, combine the dark soy sauce, fish sauce, oyster sauce and sugar in a small bowl. Set aside.

Marinate the sliced chicken in the soy sauce for at least 10 minutes.

Refresh the fresh noodles with cold water and separate the threads if needed to avoid clumping. Drain and set aside.

Heat 2 tablespoons (30 ml) of oil in a nonstick wok or large skillet over medium-high heat. Fry the chicken for about 3 minutes or until fully cooked. Transfer the cooked chicken to a bowl. Set aside.

Drizzle the remaining 2 tablespoons (30 ml) of oil in the wok and heat over medium-high. Add the garlic and cook until very aromatic. Add the egg, let set for several seconds, then scramble. Add the chopped gai lan and mix with the egg.

Add the noodles and the seasoning sauce to the pan. Stir everything quickly to ensure the noodles are fully coated with the sauce. Let the noodles sit undisturbed for about 30 seconds. You want the noodles to char a little underneath to get that caramelized flavor. Flip or toss the noodles to allow the top portion to char, too. Leave undisturbed for another 30 seconds. Return the chicken to the pan and give the mixture another quick stir. Transfer to a serving plate and sprinkle with some freshly ground pepper, to taste. Serve immediately.

MOUTHWATERING MEALS

While we usually think of rice and noodles as a side dish or accompaniment to other main dishes, there are actually many rice or noodle recipes that are substantial enough to be a stand-alone main dish. This is what makes both rice and noodles flexible, as you can enjoy them either way depending on your personal preferences. This chapter features both rice and noodles as delicious main meals as well as rice-plate combos showcasing mouthwatering fare.

Because the Philippines was under Spanish control for nearly 400 years, our cuisine has had Spanish influences. In a way, that makes our cuisine unique in Southeast Asia because we have developed a Euro–Asian culinary fusion of sorts. Such is the case with Beringhe, the local version of Spanish Paella (page 75), which uses coconut milk, ground turmeric and fish sauce for flavoring. Other dishes with Spanish influence are Arroz a la Cubana (Rice with Ground Meat, Fried Egg and Plantains, page 65) and Arroz Caldo (page 76), which means rice soup in Spanish but is essentially a Filipino congee or rice porridge with chicken and flavored with ginger.

If it's a one-pot meal you're looking for then the Chinese-style Sa Po Gai Fan (Claypot Chicken Rice, page 61), which is popular in Vietnam, Malaysia and Singapore, is a truly delicious choice. Chicken and rice seasoned with soy sauce and sesame oil are all cooked together in one pot for easy clean-up.

We do love fried chicken in Southeast Asia and Nasi Ayam Berempah (Rice with Spiced Fried Chicken, page 62) from Malaysia is pure gold and something you need to try! Perfectly spiced chicken is fried to perfection and paired with a tasty garlic and ginger rice.

If you're a fan of green curry, then Khao Pad Gang Keow Wan (Green Curry Fried Rice, page 72) is for you. With just one dish you get both a tasty curry and a rice dish that soaks up all that delicious curry-flavored sauce.

For good measure, I have added a couple of popular noodle bowl dishes from Vietnam—Bun Thịt Nuong (Rice Noodles with Grilled Pork, page 66) and Bun Cha Gio (Spring Rolls with Rice Vermicelli, page 69). The former features marinated lemongrass pork grilled to perfection and then served on top of cooked rice noodles with some herbs and greens on the side. What a show-stopping meal! The latter includes deliciously addictive crispy spring rolls, which are also great as appetizers in their own right.

You can enjoy these easy and delicious lunch and dinner ideas in no time!

SA PO GAI FAN
(Claypot Chicken Rice)

While this dish is traditionally cooked in a clay pot to achieve that crusty texture on the rice, you don't need to own a clay pot to make this easy and really tasty dish. A rice cooker or saucepan may be used and works very well, too. Whatever you use, this dish is all made in one pot for easy clean-up!

SERVES 8

2 tbsp (30 ml) dark soy sauce, divided

2 tbsp (30 ml) light (regular) soy sauce, divided

1 tbsp (15 ml) oyster sauce

3 tsp (15 ml) sesame oil, divided

1 tbsp (15 ml) freshly squeezed ginger juice

2 tsp (10 g) brown sugar

1 tsp salt

½ tsp ground white pepper

1 lb (455 g) boneless and skinless chicken breasts or thighs, cut into bite-size chunks

2 tbsp (30 ml) cooking oil of choice

2 Chinese sausages (lap cheong), soaked in hot water for 5 minutes then sliced diagonally

3 cloves garlic, peeled and crushed

2 cups (400 g) long-grain white rice like jasmine or basmati, uncooked

8 oz (225 g) fresh small shiitake mushrooms, tough ends removed then sliced in half

2½ cups (600 ml) water

3 stalks or about 2 tbsp (12 g) green onions, thinly sliced

Mix 1 tablespoon (15 ml) of the dark soy sauce, 1 tablespoon (15 ml) of the light soy sauce, the oyster sauce, 2 teaspoons (10 ml) of the sesame oil, the ginger juice, sugar, salt and white pepper in a bowl. Add the chicken and stir to fully coat. Set aside and marinate for 30 minutes.

To make drizzling sauce, combine 1 tablespoon (15 ml) of the dark soy sauce, 1 tablespoon (15 ml) of the light soy sauce and 1 teaspoon (5 ml) of the sesame oil in a small bowl. Set aside.

Heat the cooking oil over medium heat in a large clay pot or saucepan with about an 8-cup (2-L) capacity. Add the Chinese sausages and garlic and fry for 1 minute or until aromatic. Add the chicken and its marinade and cook for 3 to 4 minutes.

Add the rice, mushrooms and water and give it a quick stir. Bring the mixture to a boil, cover then simmer on low for 15 to 20 minutes, or until the rice is fully cooked and tender and the liquid has evaporated. Turn off the heat and allow the dish to sit undisturbed for another 10 minutes. Alternatively, you can also cook this in a rice cooker. If your rice cooker has a sauté function, cook as described above. When done, shift to the white rice cook setting then allow to cook until the rice is done.

Uncover and drizzle with some or all of the sauce and then mix everything together. Serve garnished with sliced green onions.

NASI AYAM BEREMPAH
(Rice with Spiced Fried Chicken)

Tender and juicy chicken pieces marinated in herbs and spices give this dish a lot of flavor and the chicken goes perfectly with a ginger- and garlic-flavored rice.

SERVES 6

5 cups (1.1 L) water

1 (3-lb [1.5-kg]) whole chicken cut up or a combination of thighs and drumsticks

8 cloves garlic, 5 cloves peeled, 3 cloves peeled and sliced

1-inch (2.5-cm) piece galangal or ginger, peeled and sliced

4 lemongrass stalks, tough outer skin removed and using only the 3–4 inch (7.5–10 cm) bottom white part, chopped

6 small shallots, peeled and chopped

1-inch (2.5-cm) piece turmeric or 1 tsp ground turmeric

1 tsp ground coriander

1 tsp ground cumin

1 tsp ground chili powder

1 tbsp (15 g) curry powder

2½ tsp (13 g) salt, divided

3 cups (600 g) long-grain white rice like jasmine, uncooked

1-inch (2.5-cm) piece ginger, peeled, chopped and smashed

2 cups (480 ml) cooking oil of choice for frying, or as needed

Sambal or chili sauce, for serving

Bring the water to a boil. Add the chicken pieces and parboil for 12 minutes. Remove the chicken and drain well. Reserve about 4 cups (1 L) of the stock.

In a food processor, grind 5 cloves of the garlic, the galangal, lemongrass, shallots and turmeric to a paste. Add a little water, about 1 tablespoon (15 ml) at a time, if needed, to keep the blades running. Spoon the mixture into a bowl.

Mix the coriander, cumin, chili powder, curry powder and 2 teaspoons (10 g) of salt. Add to the paste and mix everything to combine.

Rub the spices and paste mixture all over the chicken pieces and set aside.

Rinse the rice twice. Drain well. Place the rice in a deep saucepan. Add the stock from the boiled chicken and the 3 cloves of sliced garlic, the ginger and ½ teaspoon of salt. Bring to a boil then cover and simmer on the lowest setting for 15 to 20 minutes or until the rice is tender and the liquid has been fully absorbed. Turn off the heat and leave the rice undisturbed for 10 minutes.

Heat the oil in a frying pan to about 350°F (175°C). To test if the oil is hot enough, dip a wooden skewer, into the heated oil. When bubbles form at the end of the skewer then the oil is hot enough for frying. Fry the chicken in the oil in batches until it is golden brown and crisp. Remove the chicken from the oil and place on paper towels to drain the excess oil. You can also scoop out any additional brown bits left in the oil when you remove the chicken and set them aside with the chicken. Serve the chicken and any brown bits with the rice and sambal on the side.

ARROZ A LA CUBANA
(Rice with Ground Meat, Fried Egg and Plantains)

This tasty rice dish came to the Philippines via Spain. Filipinos, of course, gave this Cuban dish an Asian spin and use soy sauce or fish sauce to season the ground meat, which is then served with garlic fried rice, fried egg and fried plantains. A complete and delicious meal, it is popular for breakfast or lunch and can be found in most cafeterias but especially in food courts inside malls.

SERVES 4

4 cups (645 g) cooked jasmine or basmati rice, or more as needed

2 tbsp (30 ml) cooking oil of choice

3 cloves garlic, chopped

1 medium onion, chopped

2 plum tomatoes, diced

8 oz (225 g) ground beef

8 oz (225 g) ground pork

2 tbsp (30 ml) soy sauce

2 tbsp (30 ml) fish sauce

½ tsp freshly ground black pepper

1 small carrot, diced

1 red bell pepper, diced

½ cup (75 g) raisins

½ cup (75 g) frozen peas

4 fried eggs, for serving

Ripe plantains, halved then fried

Cook the rice according to the directions in the Perfect Rice recipe on page 13.

Heat the oil over medium heat in a wok or large skillet. Fry the garlic and onion for about a minute or until aromatic. Add the diced tomatoes and cook for 3 to 4 minutes or until the onion and tomatoes have softened. Stir in the ground beef and ground pork. Crumble with a fork to prevent the meat from clumping. Season with the soy sauce, fish sauce and black pepper and cook until the meat has browned all over. Add the carrot, bell pepper and raisins, then simmer covered for about 5 minutes or until the vegetables are tender.

Uncover, add the frozen peas and cook for 2 more minutes or until the peas are cooked. Transfer to a platter and keep warm.

To serve, place a cup of rice on the plate. Add a portion of the meat, a fried egg and a couple of halved fried plantains on the side. Serve immediately.

BUN THIT NUONG
(Rice Noodles with Grilled Pork)

We have a wonderful Vietnamese restaurant where we live, and my husband and I often go there to have this for lunch because it's so good! After my trip to Vietnam, I made sure I learned how to make this so I can make it in the comfort of my own home. Now you can, too! The pork can be cooked on the grill or sautéed over high heat on the stovetop. The marinade is so tasty and may be used for other types of meat, too. We have used this for beef and it came out delicious as well.

SERVES 4

For the marinade

2 tbsp (30 g) lemongrass, tough outer skin removed and using only the 3–4 inch (7.5–10 cm) bottom white part, finely chopped

1 tbsp (15 g) fresh ginger, peeled and minced

3 cloves garlic, minced

2 tbsp (30 g) sugar

1½ tbsp (23 ml) oyster sauce

1½ tbsp (23 ml) fish sauce

12 oz (345 g) boneless pork or beef, sliced into thin bite-size chunks

2 tbsp (30 ml) cooking oil

For the dressing

2 tbsp (30 ml) lime juice

2 tbsp (30 g) sugar

2 tbsp (30 ml) fish sauce

2 tbsp (30 ml) water

1 tsp garlic, minced

1 red finger-length chili, thinly sliced

For the "quick pickled" carrots and radishes

2 cups (110 g) carrots, julienned

2 cups (110 g) white radish, julienned

3 tbsp (30 g) white sugar

3 tbsp (30 ml) rice vinegar

½ tsp salt

For serving

4 oz (200 g) dried rice vermicelli

1 oz (28 g) basil leaves, for serving (optional)

1 oz (28 g) mint leaves, for serving (optional)

1 oz (28 g) shiso or tia to (purple perilla) leaves, for serving (optional)

1 small head lettuce, leaves torn, for serving

½ cup (65 g) roasted peanuts, crushed, for serving

(continued)

BUN THIT NUONG (CONTINUED)

For the marinade, mix the lemongrass, ginger, garlic, sugar, oyster sauce and fish sauce. Rub all over the pork pieces. Marinate for at least 1 hour.

For the dressing, mix the lime juice, sugar, fish sauce and water in a small bowl until the sugar is dissolved. Add the minced garlic and the chili. Set aside.

For the quick pickled carrots and radishes, mix together the carrots, white radish, sugar, rice vinegar and salt in a bowl. Set aside.

Cook the rice vermicelli in boiling water for 3 to 4 minutes, or until soft. Rinse immediately with cold water and drain well. Set aside.

You may cook the meat either by grilling or stir-frying. If grilling, thread the marinated meat on skewers and grill for about 2 to 3 minutes per side, or until done. To stir-fry, heat a wok or large skillet over high. When the wok is hot, quickly add the oil to the marinade and stir to coat the meat. Place the pork in the hot wok and stir-fry for 3 to 4 minutes or until the pork is done. Transfer to a plate.

To serve, place a portion of the cooked rice noodles into 4 bowls. On the sides surrounding the rice noodles, place any or all of the following herbs: basil, mint and shiso; then add some lettuce, carrots and radish. Place a few pieces of the cooked pork in the middle. Garnish with some crushed nuts and serve the dressing on the side. It's a good idea to pour a little bit of dressing over the salad as you eat, according to taste. This way, it won't make the salad soggy and you can enjoy all the complex flavors of the dish with every bite!

NOTE: Finely chopped lemongrass may be purchased frozen in some Asian stores. Simply thaw before using. However, fresh lemongrass adds more flavor and aroma, so use it if it's available.

BUN CHA GIO
(Spring Rolls with Rice Vermicelli)

I love Vietnamese noodle bowls and I could seriously eat one every day and never get tired of them! Thankfully, there are many varieties of these noodle bowls and this one is an easy favorite. Crispy spring rolls filled with perfectly seasoned ground pork are sliced into pieces and then eaten with some salad greens, fresh herbs and rice noodles (of course!). The special dressing is sweet, salty, sour and garlicky with a little spicy kick, and it adds so much flavor to this dish!

SERVES 4

For the spring rolls

1 lb (455 g) ground pork

3 cloves garlic, minced

1 onion, finely chopped

4 dried wood ear mushrooms, rehydrated in hot water for 15 minutes, tough parts removed, then finely chopped

½ cup (55 g) carrots, minced

2½ oz (68 g) glass noodles, soaked in water for 30 minutes or until soft, trimmed into shorter lengths

1 egg, beaten

1 tbsp (15 ml) fish sauce

1 tbsp (15 ml) oyster sauce

1 tsp sugar

½ tsp salt

½ tsp ground pepper

28 (8 x 8–inch [20 x 20–cm]) thin spring roll wrappers or pastry sheets

2 cups (480 ml) cooking oil, for deep frying

For the dipping sauce

2 tbsp (30 ml) fish sauce

2 tbsp (30 ml) freshly squeezed lime juice

2 tbsp (30 ml) sugar

2 tbsp (30 ml) water

1 clove garlic, minced

1–2 finger-length red chilis, thinly sliced

For the noodle bowl

8 oz (225 g) dried rice vermicelli, cooked in boiling water for 3 to 4 minutes or until soft, rinsed and drained well

1 oz (28 g) mint leaves, chopped

1 oz (28 g) tia to or shiso leaves (red perilla), chopped

1 cucumber, sliced

1 small head of lettuce, torn

Handful of quick pickled carrots and radishes (see recipe on page 66)

(continued)

BUN CHA GIO (CONTINUED)

Mix together the ground pork, garlic, onion, mushrooms, carrots, noodles and egg. Season with the fish sauce, oyster sauce, sugar, salt and pepper. Mix everything well using your hands.

To make the spring rolls, place about 2 tablespoons (30 g) of the filling in one of the corners of the wrapper. Roll the corner with the filling (spreading it a little) toward the middle of the wrapper. Fold the sides inward to seal, then continue to roll until you have about 2 inches (5 cm) left of the wrapper. Using your finger, brush the edges with a little water and then seal completely. Make sure it is tightly secured. Place the finished roll on a platter with the sealed side downward. Repeat until all of the filling is used.

Heat the oil in a saucepan to medium or about 350°F (175°C). To test if the oil is hot enough, dip a wooden skewer deep into the oil. When bubbles begin to form at the tip of the skewer, the oil is ready for frying. Fry the spring rolls in batches, avoiding overcrowding, for about 4 to 5 minutes or until golden brown all over.

For the dipping sauce, mix the fish sauce, lime juice, sugar and water in a small bowl until the sugar is fully dissolved. Add the minced garlic and sliced chilis.

Divide the noodles into bowls. Place the chopped herbs, cucumber and lettuce greens around the edge of the bowl surrounding the noodles. Chop two or three spring rolls and place on top of the noodles. Serve with the sauce on the side. It's best to drizzle the sauce a little at a time as you eat the salad.

NOTE: The spring rolls (Cha Gio) also may be served on their own or added to noodle bowls such as the Bun Thit Nuong (page 66).

KHAO PAD GANG KEOW WAN
(Green Curry Fried Rice)

If you are a big fan of Thai Green Curry, then this rice dish is for you. It has all the tastes and aroma of your favorite green curry with the rice soaking up all that delicious flavor. It truly is a green curry dish, but in fried-rice form. You can make it with chicken, pork or shrimp. Best of all, it's a one-pot wonder and, certainly, a meal on its own.

SERVES 4

3 cups (480 g) cooked, cold long-grain jasmine rice (preferably leftover)

2 tbsp (30 ml) cooking oil of choice

1–1½ tbsp (15–23 g) green curry paste (see Note)

1 cup (125 g) chicken breasts or boneless skinless thighs, sliced into small pieces

½ cup (120 ml) coconut milk

5 kaffir lime leaves, rolled up and then thinly sliced

3 Thai eggplants, quartered and then halved

1 long and mild red chili or red Fresno pepper

2 tbsp (30 ml) fish sauce

1 tbsp (13 g) sugar

1 cup (150 g) frozen peas

¼ cup (10 g) Thai basil or regular basil leaves

Salt, to taste

Dampen your hands with a little water, then rub the rice between your fingers to separate the grains. Place the rice in a bowl and set aside.

Heat the oil and curry paste in a pan over medium heat. Fry the paste for 30 seconds, or until aromatic. Add the chicken and increase the heat to medium-high and cook for 2 minutes or until the meat turns white. Pour in the coconut milk and add the kaffir lime leaves and simmer briefly, for 1 minute or less. Add the eggplant, red chili, fish sauce and sugar then simmer for another 2 minutes or until the vegetables are tender and the chicken is fully cooked.

Turn up the heat again to medium-high then add the rice and cook until most of the liquid has been absorbed by the rice and it's fully heated through. Add the frozen peas and continue to cook for another minute. Then stir in the basil leaves and stir-fry until the basil leaves have just wilted. Taste and adjust the seasoning with a little salt if needed. Serve immediately.

NOTE: If your curry paste is mild, feel free to increase the amount to the spice level you prefer.

BERINGHE
(Filipino-Style Paella)

This is another recipe via Spain that the Filipinos have adapted as their own. In the Philippines this is described as the poor man's version of paella. But don't be deceived, although it's not as expensive to make as its Spanish counterpart it certainly won't be beaten in flavor! With a bright yellow color from turmeric, this rice is cooked in seasoned coconut milk and loaded with tender chicken pieces and your favorite vegetables. This dish is great for a crowd!

SERVES 8 TO 10

2 cups (400 g) sticky or glutinous white rice

1 tbsp (15 ml) cooking oil of choice

3 Spanish chorizo sausages, sliced (optional)

3 cloves garlic, minced

1 shallot, finely chopped

1 lb (455 g) boneless, skinless chicken breasts or thighs cut into bite-size pieces and seasoned with 1 tsp (5 g) salt

1 tbsp (15 g) ground turmeric dissolved in 2 tbsp (30 ml) warm water

1 (13.5-oz [400-ml]) can coconut milk

1½ cups (360 ml) chicken stock

2 pandan leaves, tied into a knot (optional)

1 red bell pepper, chopped, divided

1 cup (150 g) raisins

1 cups (160 g) cooked white rice

2 tbsp (30 ml) fish sauce, or more to taste

1 cup (150 g) fresh or frozen green peas

Salt, to taste

Hard-boiled eggs, halved, for serving

Soak the sticky rice in water for 1 to 2 hours before cooking. Rinse and drain well.

Heat the oil over medium heat in a nonstick wok or large skillet. Fry the chorizo slices, if using, for about 2 to 3 minutes or until they have crisped up, turned deep red and released their oil. Transfer to a plate and set aside. In the same pan, stir-fry the garlic and shallot for about a minute or until aromatic. Add the chicken and the turmeric dissolved in water. Stir and cook for 3 to 4 minutes. Add the drained sticky rice to the pan. Stir-fry for 2 to 3 minutes or until heated through and the rice is fully coated with the turmeric.

Pour in the the coconut milk, chicken stock and the pandan leaves, if using. Allow the mixture to come to a boil then cover and simmer on low for 15 minutes. When the coconut milk has reduced and the mixture has thickened, add the chorizo and half of the bell pepper and the raisins and continue to cook until the rice is fully tender. Add the cooked white rice and season with the fish sauce. Mix well. Add the green peas and cook for another minute. Taste and adjust seasoning with extra salt or fish sauce if desired.

Remove the pandan leaves if they were used. Serve with the hard-boiled eggs and top with the remaining bell pepper. Serve immediately.

ARROZ CALDO
(Rice Soup with Chicken)

In Spanish this dish literally means "rice soup," but despite its European-sounding nomenclature, this dish is Asian through and through and is in fact of Chinese origin. This Filipino version of a congee or rice porridge has stewed chicken and lots of ginger which makes this soup zesty and delicious! While this soup is usually served at breakfast or lunch, it is also often made when someone is sick because it's a soothing and tasty soup that's easy on the stomach. Truly a chicken soup for the weary soul!

SERVES 8

1 tbsp (15 ml) cooking oil of choice

6 cloves garlic, minced

1 onion, finely chopped

¼ cup (32 g) fresh ginger, peeled and sliced into thin strips

3 lb (1.4 kg) chicken, cut up into serving pieces

3 tbsp (45 ml) fish sauce

1 cup (200 g) uncooked white rice (like jasmine)

½ cup (100 g) uncooked sticky or glutinous white rice

4 cups (1 L) chicken stock

4 cups (1 L) water

Salt and pepper, to taste

Green onions, thinly sliced, for serving

Fried minced garlic, for serving

Lemon or lime slices, for serving

In a large soup pot or deep saucepan, heat the oil over medium heat. Stir-fry the garlic, onion and ginger for 3 minutes until very fragrant. Add the chicken pieces and season with the fish sauce. Cook for a couple of minutes. Adjust the heat to medium-low, cover and cook for 15 to 20 minutes or until the chicken releases its fat.

Add both the regular and sticky rice, stir and cook for another minute. Pour in the chicken stock and water and bring to a boil. Simmer uncovered and cook until the rice is tender and the soup has turned into a thick porridge. Taste and adjust the seasoning with salt and pepper if needed. Ladle the soup into individual bowls, and garnish with green onions and fried minced garlic. Squeeze in a few drops of lemon or lime juice for extra tang before eating!

SATISFYING SOUPS

When I began writing this book, a chapter for soup wasn't originally included as I thought I could just add a few soups here and there in other chapters. But as I did my research and traveled around Southeast Asia, I realized I needed to make an entire chapter just for soup as there are so many delicious soup recipes out there that I didn't want any of you to miss.

In Southeast Asia, it's pretty common to begin the day with a soup, so a congee or Asian porridge made from rice is very typical. This is pretty much our oatmeal! The Vietnamese Chao Hai San (Rice Soup with Seafood, page 91) will not only fill you up but will also delight your taste buds with its delicious combination of shrimp, fish and mushrooms. The mushrooms add extra meaty texture and umami flavors to the dish.

For beef and noodle lovers, the classic Pho Bo (Noodle Soup with Beef, page 87) from Vietnam and Pares Mami (Filipino Beef Noodle Soup, page 81) from the Philippines—both meaty, perfectly spiced and seasoned—will make you go for second or third bowls. Don't worry, both recipes make huge batches so there's plenty for everyone! If beef is not your favorite, simply replace with chicken.

One of the soups I grew up eating is Misua Sopas (Thin Wheat Noodle Soup with Meatballs, page 95). Misua are really thin noodles that cook instantly when they are mixed with the broth. We probably had this soup several times a month because it's so tasty and so perfect with rice. Yes, it's not odd to enjoy both rice and noodles together and this soup will prove that!

And for those who love curry-based soups, the Laksa (Coconut Curry Noodle Soup, page 99), Khao Soy Gai (Curry Noodle Soup with Chicken, page 85) and Lontong Sayur Lodeh (Compressed Rice with Vegetables in Coconut Broth, page 92) won't disappoint. All braised in a creamy coconut milk sauce yet with their own distinct flavors, ingredients and spice level, you'll be mopping up every drop of sauce in each bowl.

Showcasing a delicious blend of sour, salty, spicy and literally hot, the Tom Yum (Hot and Sour Soup, page 82) from Thailand won't disappoint.

Don't worry, I didn't forget to add some delightful chicken noodle soups to the mix. There's the comforting bowl of Soto Ayam (Chicken Noodle Soup with Tumeric and Ginger, page 96) from Indonesia and Sotanghon Sopas (Glass Noodle Soup with Chicken, page 100) from the Philippines, either of which you can happily slurp!

PARES MAMI
(Filipino Beef Noodle Soup)

This is the Filipino version of pho and is equally tasty. Tender pieces of beef are cooked slowly until meltingly tender in a perfectly seasoned and spiced broth. Fresh egg noodles are then added to make a mouthwateringly delicious soup that is perfect for the entire family!

SERVES 6

2 tbsp (30 ml) cooking oil of choice

6 cloves garlic, peeled and crushed

2.2 lb (1 kg) chuck roast or beef brisket, cut into bite-size cubes and seasoned with 1 tsp each of salt and pepper

4 cups (1 L) beef broth or beef stock

4 cups (1 L) water

2 cinnamon sticks

6 star anise

1½ tbsp (23 ml) soy sauce, or to taste

1½ tbsp (23 g) sugar

Salt and pepper, to taste

1 (1-lb [455-g]) package cooked egg or mami noodles, blanched briefly in hot water then drained

Napa or Savoy cabbage, shredded coleslaw style

Green onions, sliced thinly

Hard-boiled eggs, peeled and halved, for serving

Fried garlic, for serving

Red chili, sliced, for serving (optional)

Lime slices, for serving

Heat the oil in a stock pot over medium heat. Add the garlic and cook for 1 minute or until aromatic. Add the beef cubes and cook for 20 minutes, turning the meat halfway through the cooking time, until the beef is browned all over and has released its fat. Add the beef broth and water to the pan, then add the cinnamon sticks and star anise. Bring to a boil, then lower the heat to a simmer. Cover and cook until the meat is tender, between 1½ and 2 hours. Season the broth with the soy sauce, sugar and salt and pepper, to taste.

Ladle the noodles into individual bowls and top with a portion of the cabbage and green onions. Then ladle the hot soup and beef cubes on top. Add the egg and garnish with the fried garlic and red chili, if using. Serve with lime slices on the side.

TOM YUM
(Hot and Sour Soup)

This noodle soup with prawns is sour, spicy, savory and easy to make. With flavors from lemongrass, kaffir lime leaves, galangal and a homemade prawn stock, it is deliciously comforting. The addition of egg or wheat noodles makes it the perfect meal in a bowl.

SERVES 4 TO 6

1 lb (455 g) raw prawns or shrimps

1 tbsp (15 ml) cooking oil of choice

2 tbsp (30 g) dried shrimp

6 cups (1.5 L) water

1 tsp salt, or to taste

3 stalks lemongrass, tough outer layer removed and using only the 3–4 inch (7.5–10 cm) bottom white part, bruised

1-inch (2.5-cm) piece galangal, peeled and sliced

6 kaffir lime leaves, torn

2 tbsp (6 g) fresh cilantro or coriander, roots and stems, plus chopped leaves for garnish

1 finger-length red chili, thinly sliced

8 oz (225 g) fresh egg or wheat noodles (wonton noodles)

1½ cups (165 g) button mushrooms, sliced

2 plum tomatoes, quartered

2–3 tbsp (30–45 ml) fish sauce, or to taste

2–3 tbsp (30–45 ml) tamarind paste, or to taste

Juice of 1 lime or about 2 tbsp (30 ml)

Peel the prawns and reserve the heads. Rinse the peeled prawns and set aside.

Heat the oil over medium-high heat in a soup pot. Fry the prawn heads and dried shrimp in the oil for 1 to 2 minutes, or until the shells change color. Pour in the water, bring to a boil, then reduce the heat to a simmer and cook for 15 minutes. Season with the salt. Strain the stock with a fine sieve and discard the solids. This stock can be made ahead, if preferred.

Bring the strained stock, lemongrass, galangal, lime leaves, cilantro and red chili to a boil. Lower the heat and simmer for 5 minutes. Add the noodles, prawns, mushrooms and tomatoes and cook for another 3 minutes or until the prawns have just turned opaque and bright pink and the noodles are softened. Season with the fish sauce, tamarind paste and lime juice. Adjust the seasoning, if needed. The soup should be sour, spicy and savory.

Ladle into bowls and garnish with some chopped cilantro on top.

KHAO SOY GAI
(Curry Noodle Soup with Chicken)

Sweet, creamy, aromatic and mildly spiced this egg noodles in chicken curry soup is the perfect example of what comfort food is all about. This is so delicious that even my kids who aren't into anything curry or spicy totally love this dish!

SERVES 4 TO 6

For the nam prik gaeng khao soy (khao soy curry paste)

1 dried, long red chili or Fresno red pepper

1-inch (2.5-cm) piece ginger, peeled and sliced

2 tsp (10 g) yellow curry powder

2 fresh coriander or cilantro roots (about 1 tbsp [2.5 g]) (see Notes)

2 tsp (10 g) ground turmeric or 1-inch (2.5-cm) piece fresh turmeric

2 shallots, peeled

3 garlic cloves, peeled

½ tsp salt

1 tbsp (15 g) Thai shrimp paste

For the soup

2 tbsp (30 ml) cooking oil of choice

1 (13.5-oz [400-ml]) can coconut cream

1 lb (455 g) chicken thighs and drumsticks, lightly seasoned with salt and pepper

2 tbsp (25 g) palm or light brown sugar

1½ tbsp (23 ml) fish sauce, plus more to taste

1 cup (240 ml) coconut milk or coconut cream

Salt, to taste

1 lb (455 g) fresh egg noodles (wonton noodles), divided

1½ cups (360 ml) cooking oil of choice, for frying

Lime, sliced, for serving

Fried shallots, for serving

Fresh cilantro or coriander leaves, for serving

To make the paste, soak the dried chili in very hot water for 10 minutes or until rehydrated. Slice lengthwise and deseed. In a mortar and pestle or food processor grind the chili, ginger, curry powder, coriander roots, turmeric, shallots, garlic and salt to a smooth paste. Add the shrimp paste to the spice paste and mix well.

In a wok or large pot, heat the oil over medium-low heat and add the curry paste and cook, stirring occasionally, for 2 to 3 minutes, or until fragrant. Pour in the coconut cream and bring to a boil.

Add the chicken, sugar and fish sauce. Stir. Cover and simmer for another 30 to 40 minutes or until the chicken pieces are cooked and tender. Uncover and add the coconut milk. Bring to a boil, then simmer for 1 minute. Taste and adjust the seasoning with a little salt or fish sauce if needed. The sauce should be sweet, very slightly salty and mildly spiced. Keep the curry soup warm as you prepare the noodles and other accompaniments.

(continued)

KHAO SOY GAI (CONTINUED)

Separate out about a quarter of the noodles to make the fried topping. Heat the oil in a saucepan to about 350°F (175°C). Fry a small portion of the noodles one at a time for 2 to 3 seconds or just until crispy and creamy in color. This happens very quickly and the noodles shouldn't turn brown. Repeat with the remaining quarter of the noodles. Set the fried noodles aside.

Blanch the remaining egg noodles briefly in boiling water for 1 minute or until cooked through, then drain. Divide the blanched noodles among the bowls.

Ladle the chicken curry on top of the cooked noodles. Top with the deep fried egg noodles. Garnish with lime slices, fried shallots and some chopped fresh cilantro or coriander.

NOTES: Pounding ingredients in a mortar and pestle to make a paste may sound tedious, but it's worth the effort as it allows the release of flavor, color and oil from the spice ingredients, which will make your dish even more flavorful. I personally find it therapeutic, so why not try it?

Cilantro or fresh coriander with roots may be purchased in the produce section of any Asian grocery store. The roots of cilantro actually provide a lot of flavor to many Southeast Asian dishes, so they are never thrown away and discarded.

PHO BO
(Noodle Soup with Beef)

Pho, the classic Vietnamese soup, needs no lengthy introduction as it speaks for itself. This soup offers a perfectly spiced and seasoned beef broth made from scratch served with rice noodles and thinly sliced beef, then garnished with fresh coriander and bean sprouts and served with lime, hoisin sauce and chili sauce on the side. The ultimate comfort food in a bowl! I learned how to make the most delicious pho through the help of Chef Tan Viet Luong from Ho Chi Minh, Vietnam, so I am indebted to him for this delicious recipe. Chicken may be used instead of beef.

SERVES 6 TO 8

4.4 lb (2 kg) beef bones

2 oz (50 g) whole fresh ginger

1 large yellow onion, skin on

3 star anise

9 whole cloves

9 black peppercorns

3 cinnamon sticks

3 cardamom pods

1 lb (455 g) beef brisket or chuck roast

10 cups (2.5 L) water, or more as needed

3 tbsp (45 ml) fish sauce

3 tbsp (45 g) sugar

1 tbsp (15 g) salt

2.2 lbs (1 kg) fresh rice noodles or 1 lb (455 g) dried rice noodles

2 cups (120 g) bean sprouts

8 oz (225 g) raw beef filet, like beef tenderloin or beef sirloin, shaved or cut into paper-thin slices

3 stalks or about 2 tbsp (12 g) green onions, thinly sliced

Fresh cilantro, for serving

2 red chilis, thinly sliced

Fresh mint leaves, for serving

Basil leaves, for serving

Limes, sliced into wedges, for serving

Hoisin sauce, for serving

Chili sauce, for serving

In a soup or deep pot place the beef bones with enough water to cover the bones. Bring to a boil and cook for about 3 minutes. Drain, then rinse the bones with fresh water. Set aside.

Over an open flame, roast the ginger and the onion until the skin turns dark brown. Alternatively, slice the ginger and onion in half, then roast in a preheated 350°F (175°C) oven for 30 minutes.

Toast the star anise, cloves, black peppercorns, cinnamon sticks and cardamom pods for 1 minute over medium heat in a frying pan, or until fragrant. Place in a small spice fabric bag or cheesecloth and tie with a string to make a small pouch to hold the spices.

(continued)

PHO BO (CONTINUED)

Place the rinsed bones, roasted ginger and onion, beef brisket and the spice bag into a deep soup pot. Pour the water into the pot, bring to a boil, then cover and adjust the heat to low and simmer for at least 4 hours. Remove the beef brisket after 1½ hours or when it's fork tender. Allow the brisket to cool, then slice into strips. Set aside. After the rest of the broth has been simmering for 4 hours or so, strain the stock with a fine sieve to obtain a clear soup (measure between about 8 to 9 cups [1.9 to 2.2 L] of stock). Place the strained stock and the brisket in a new clean pot. Bring to a boil, then simmer over low heat and season with the fish sauce, sugar and salt. Taste and adjust the seasoning if desired. Keep the stock hot.

If using dried rice noodles, cook the noodles in boiling water for 3 to 4 minutes or until soft. Rinse in cold water and drain well. If using fresh rice noodles, simply blanch in hot water very briefly, for 2 to 4 seconds. Drain. Do this in individual batches or portions. Quickly blanch the bean sprouts.

Place a portion of the noodles and bean sprouts in each bowl. Top with very thin slices of raw beef filet, green onions and fresh cilantro, then add the hot stock and brisket. Serve with the red chilis, a few mint leaves, basil leaves, some lime slices and hoisin sauce and chili sauce on the side.

CHAO HAI SAN

(Rice Soup with Seafood)

Some congees or rice porridges can be bland and tasteless, but not this one! Loaded with seafood and mushrooms, then seasoned with fish sauce and mushroom powder, you won't believe rice porridge can be this good!

SERVES 8

1 cup (200 g) broken or regular jasmine rice

10 cups (2.5 L) water, divided

2 tbsp (30 ml) cooking oil of choice

3 cloves garlic, minced

1 shallot, finely chopped

8 oz (225 g) prawns or shrimps, peeled and deveined, then finely chopped

6 oz (130 g) white flesh fish, finely chopped

8 oz (225 g) fresh shiitake mushrooms, thinly sliced

1 cup (110 g) carrots, minced

4 tbsp (60 ml) fish sauce

2 tbsp (30 g) mushroom seasoning powder or granules

2 tbsp (30 g) sugar

Salt and pepper, to taste

Green onions, sliced thinly, for serving

Fresh cilantro or coriander, coarsely chopped, for serving

Add the rice to a deep pan and heat over medium heat. Toast the rice, stirring frequently, for 4 to 5 minutes or until the grains turn creamy in color.

Pour in 8 cups (2 L) of water and simmer over low heat for about 1 hour or until most of the liquid has been absorbed by the rice and it has the consistency of porridge.

In a wok or large skillet, heat the oil over medium heat. Add the garlic and shallot and fry for about 30 seconds or until very aromatic. Add the prawns, fish, mushrooms and carrots and cook for 2 to 3 minutes, stirring often. Season with the fish sauce, mushroom seasoning powder and sugar, then stir.

Transfer the contents of the wok to the rice and mix to combine. Pour in the remaining 2 cups (480 ml) of water. Turn up the heat to bring the porridge to a simmer. Cook for another 5 minutes, or until the porridge thickens. Taste and season with salt and pepper if needed.

Serve each bowl garnished with chopped green onion and cilantro.

NOTE: Mushroom powder is made from dried mushrooms. You can make your own, if you wish, as it is such a delicious food enhancer and is a good substitute for the dreaded monosodium glutamate (MSG). However, you can also purchase this in Asian stores or online. Buy a mushroom powder that is pure and not laden with MSG or other additives.

LONTONG SAYUR LODEH
(Compressed Rice with Vegetables in Coconut Broth)

This tasty curry-flavored soup can be made fully vegetarian and is the perfect vehicle for ketupat (compressed rice cakes), which are added to the soup just before serving. Noodles may also be added for a truly substantial and delicious meal.

SERVES 6

2 tbsp (30 g) dried shrimp

1 cup (240 ml) boiling water

2 finger-length red chilis, seeded

2 long red chilis or Fresno red peppers, seeded

6 small shallots, peeled

3 cloves garlic, peeled

6 candlenuts or macadamia nuts

1-inch (2.5-cm) piece galangal, peeled and chopped

3 tbsp (45 ml) cooking oil of choice

2 tsp (10 g) ground turmeric, dissolved in 1½ cups (360 ml) water

6 kaffir lime leaves, torn

1 cup (110 g) carrots, julienned

1 cup (98 g) Chinese long beans or green beans, sliced into 1-inch (2.5-cm) pieces

1 tbsp (13 g) brown sugar

1½ tsp (8 g) salt

2 cups (106 g) Napa or Savoy cabbage (about a quarter of a large head), coarsely chopped

1 lb (455 g) prawns or shrimps, peeled and deveined with the tails on

1 (13.5-oz [400-ml]) can coconut milk

Ketupat (page 22), cubed

Hard-boiled eggs, for serving

Fried shallots, for serving

Sambal or chili paste, for serving

Rehydrate the dried shrimp in hot water for 15 minutes. Drain the shrimp through a fine strainer and reserve the water and shrimp separately. Set aside.

Using a mortar and pestle or food processor, grind the chilis, shallots, garlic, nuts, galangal and rehydrated shrimp to a smooth paste. If using a food processor, add 1 to 2 tablespoons (15 to 30 ml) of reserved shrimp water to the spices to allow the blade to spin if needed.) It is best to grind the spices with a mortar and pestle to release their natural oil, colors and flavors, so use this method if possible.

Heat the oil over medium-low heat. Fry the chili paste for 6 to 8 minutes or until the paste has darkened and has began to release its oil.

Pour in the remaining reserved shrimp water and the ground turmeric dissolved in water. Scrape up any brown bits at the bottom of the pan. Increase the heat and bring the mixture to a boil, then add the kaffir lime leaves, carrots, long beans, sugar and salt. Cover and simmer for 2 to 3 minutes, or until the vegetables are tender but not mushy. Add the cabbage, prawns and coconut milk and simmer for another 3 to 4 minutes or until the prawns and cabbage are fully cooked. Taste the soup and add more salt or sugar, if needed. It should be spicy and savory with a hint of sweetness.

To serve, divide the cubed ketupat among the serving bowls. Ladle the soup on top and garnish with the halved hard-boiled eggs and fried shallots. Serve with sambal on the side.

MISUA SOPAS
(Thin Wheat Noodle Soup with Meatballs)

Misua (mee sua or miswa) are very thin noodle threads made from wheat. These noodles cook very fast so they're ideal to add to soups at the end of cooking. My favorite use for misua is in a soup with meatballs, eaten with plain rice and some fish sauce on the side. A piping hot bowl of tasty misua soup is perfect for those fall and winter chilly nights.

SERVES 6

1 lb (455 g) ground pork

1 egg, lightly beaten

½ cup (55 g) carrots, grated

3 stalks or about 2 tbsp (12 g) green onions, thinly sliced, plus more for serving

1 tbsp (15 ml) soy sauce

½ tbsp (8 g) freshly grated ginger

1 tsp brown sugar

1 tsp salt, plus more to taste

½ tsp ground pepper

3 tbsp (45 ml) cooking oil of choice

3 cloves garlic, sliced

1 onion, chopped

2-inch (5-cm) piece ginger, peeled and sliced (see Notes)

4 cups (1 L) chicken stock

4 cups (1 L) water

1 patola or loofah/luffa gourd, peeled then sliced

2 tbsp (30 ml) fish sauce, or to taste

8 oz (225 g) dried misua (thin dried wheat noodles)

In a large bowl, mix together by hand the ground pork, egg, carrots, green onions, soy sauce, ginger, sugar, salt and pepper. Shape the ground meat mixture into 1-inch (2.5-cm) balls.

Heat the oil over medium heat in a deep pan or soup pot. Sear the meatballs in batches until nicely browned all over. Set aside. In the same pan, sauté the garlic, onion and ginger for 2 minutes or until very aromatic. Pour in the chicken stock and water and bring to a boil. Scrape any brown bits at the bottom. Return the meatballs to the pan and simmer for 15 minutes. Add the sliced patola and fish sauce and simmer until the vegetables are tender. Taste and adjust the seasoning with extra salt if needed.

Blanch the misua noodles in hot water briefly. These noodles are so thin that they will soften immediately. Ladle some noodles into each bowl and then add the meatballs and vegetables and some hot broth. Garnish with some chopped green onions.

NOTES: Adding the cooked noodles to individual bowls will ensure that the noodles don't over-soak in the soup and get mushy. However, if you're planning to serve the soup immediately, you can simply add the noodles straight to the soup.

The best way to peel the ginger is by using a teaspoon. Using a spoon allows you to scrape off the ginger flesh easily and to reach into the hidden crevices of this aromatic spice.

SOTO AYAM
(Chicken Noodle Soup with Turmeric and Ginger)

Soto Ayam is great to feed to a crowd because it can be made ahead and assembled later on when it's serving time. The homemade broth is the star here, with flavors from garlic, ginger, lemongrass and kaffir lime leaves—it's not only very aromatic, the taste is outstanding, too!

SERVES 6 TO 8

3–4 lb (1.5–2 kg) whole chicken, cut up (see Note)

6 cups (1.5 L) water

3 stalks lemongrass, tough outer layer removed and using only the 3–4 inch (7.5–10 cm) bottom white part, bruised

6 kaffir lime leaves, torn

3 stalks or about 2 tbsp (12 g) green onions, sliced into 1-inch (2.5-cm) pieces

1 celery stick, sliced

2 tsp (10 g) salt, divided

8 cloves garlic, peeled

1-inch (2.5-cm) piece turmeric, peeled

1-inch (2.5-cm) piece ginger, peeled

1 tbsp (15 ml) cooking oil of choice

8 oz (225 g) dried glass noodles or mung bean threads

2 cups (106 g) bean sprouts

Hard-boiled eggs, peeled and halved, for serving

Fried shallots, for serving

Green onions, sliced thinly, for serving

Lime slices, for serving

Sweet soy sauce, for serving

Sambal or chili sauce, for serving

Place the cut-up chicken in a deep pan with the water and add the lemongrass, kaffir lime leaves, green onions, celery and 1½ teaspoons (9 g) of salt. Bring to a boil, then turn down to simmer over low heat.

In a food processor or using a mortar and pestle, grind the garlic, turmeric, ginger and ½ teaspoon of salt to make a paste. Heat the oil over low to medium heat in another pan and fry the paste until it is fragrant, for 1 to 2 minutes. Add the paste to the simmering chicken broth and stir well. Cover the broth and continue to simmer for 30 to 40 minutes or until the chicken is fully cooked.

Remove the chicken when done and discard the skin and bones. Shred the meat and set aside. Strain the broth and reserve the liquid.

Cook the glass noodles in boiling water for 3 to 4 minutes or until soft. Drain and trim into short lengths. Blanch the bean sprouts.

To serve, place a portion of the glass noodles in each bowl, then add the blanched bean sprouts and shredded chicken. Pour enough broth into each bowl to soak most of the ingredients. Top with the hard-boiled eggs, fried shallots and green onions. Serve with the lime, sweet soy sauce and sambal or chili sauce on the side.

NOTE: For a shortcut in this recipe, use plain roasted chicken. Take the breast, thighs and drumstick meat and cut into small pieces or simply shred the meat. Set aside the shredded meat. Add all the bones and cook the broth as above and proceed with the rest of the instructions. If desired, you can set aside a portion of the chicken like the breast and sauté pieces of it with a little garlic, salt and ground tumeric. Use this as topping—it will add a pop of color to the soup.

LAKSA
(Coconut Curry Noodle Soup)

Laksa is a delicious soup loaded with rice noodles and seafood or poultry in a rich and perfectly spiced coconut curry broth. It's filling and satisfying, so one bowl is good enough for a meal.

SERVES 4 TO 6

¼ cup (13 g) dried anchovies

1 (13.5-oz [400-ml]) can coconut milk

2 long red chilis, seeded

4 cloves garlic, peeled

6 small shallots

1-inch (2.5-cm) piece ginger, peeled

6 candlenuts or macadamia nuts

1 tsp (5 g) dried shrimp paste (belacan), toasted

2 tbsp (5 g) mint, sliced

1½ tbsp (23 g) red curry powder, or to taste

1 tbsp (15 ml) sambal or chili paste or sauce

2 tbsp (30 ml) cooking oil of choice

1-inch (2.5-cm) piece galangal, peeled and bruised

4 stalks lemongrass, tough outer layer removed and using only the bottom white part, bruised

½–1 cup (120–240 ml) water, or as needed

7 oz (198 g) fried or puffed tofu

1 tbsp (15 g) sugar, or more to taste

2 tsp (10 g) salt, or more to taste

8 oz (225 g) dried rice noodles, cooked according to package directions then drained

8 oz (225 g) prawns or shrimps, cooked

2 cups (120 g) bean sprouts, blanched briefly

Hard-boiled eggs, for serving

Red chilis, thinly sliced, for serving

Fried shallots, for serving

Lime or calamansi slices, for serving

Mix the anchovies into the coconut milk and set aside.

Make the spice paste by grinding the red chilis, garlic, shallots, ginger, candlenuts, shrimp paste and mint in a mortar and pestle or food processor. Place the paste in a bowl and mix with the red curry and sambal.

Heat the oil in a saucepan over medium heat. Fry the bruised galangal and lemongrass until fragrant. Add the prepared laksa paste, adjust the heat to low, then cook for 6 to 8 minutes or until the paste darkens in color and begins to release its oil.

Slowly add the coconut milk with the anchovies, the water and the fried tofu. Bring the mixture to a boil then lower the heat to a simmer. Add the sugar and season with salt, to taste. Keep the soup hot as you prepare the other ingredients for serving. Before serving remove the galangal and lemongrass.

To serve, ladle the hot curry soup into bowls, then add the cooked rice noodles, prawns and bean sprouts. Garnish with a hard-boiled egg and some chili slices, fried shallots and a slice of lime.

NOTES: Dried anchovies can be found in Asian stores. Belacan (dried shrimp paste) needs to be toasted before using to release its flavor. Dry fry a small portion in a shallow pan until it because pungent and powdery. Use as seasoning for your soups or stews.

You can buy ready-made sambal or chili paste or sauce in Asian stores or you can make your own by rehydrating dried red chilis in boiling water for 10 to 15 minutes or until they turn soft, then grinding them to a paste.

SOTANGHON SOPAS

(Glass Noodle Soup with Chicken)

This noodle soup features a tasty broth with chicken, glass noodles and mushrooms. At home we love to have this with a plate of rice, but it can certainly be enjoyed as a meal on its own. It is one of those go-to foods whenever you need a delicious bowl of soup.

SERVES 6 TO 8

6 oz (170 g) dried sotanghon (glass noodles or mung bean thread)

8–10 dried shiitake mushrooms, rehydrated then sliced

4 cups (1 L) hot water

4 cups (1 L) chicken stock

3 lb (1.5 kg) whole chicken, cut into pieces (see Note)

3 onions, 2 peeled and quartered and 1 peeled and chopped

3 bay leaves

1 tbsp (15 g) whole peppercorns

3 tbsp (45 ml) fish sauce, divided

2 tbsp (30 ml) cooking oil of choice

3 cloves garlic, minced

2 tbsp (30 g) mushroom powder seasoning

Salt and white ground pepper, to taste

3 stalks or about 2 tbsp (12 g) green onions, thinly sliced

Soak the sotanghon in room-temperature water for 20 minutes or until soft. Drain, trim to shorten and set aside.

Soak the dried shiitake mushrooms in 4 cups (1 L) of hot water for 20 to 30 minutes or until soft. Drain and reserve the water. Remove the stem or tough part of the mushrooms then slice.

In a soup pot, bring the chicken stock and reserved mushroom water to a boil. Add the chicken pieces, 2 quartered onions, bay leaves, whole peppercorns and 1 tablespoon (15 ml) of fish sauce. Lower the heat and simmer, covered, for 50 to 60 minutes or until the chicken pieces are tender and fully cooked.

Remove the chicken, strain the stock and discard the solids. When the chicken is cool enough to handle, discard the bones and skin and shred the meat.

In the same pot, heat the oil over medium heat. Fry the garlic and 1 chopped onion for about 1 minute or until aromatic. Add the shredded chicken and mushrooms and stir-fry for 2 to 3 minutes. Add the strained stock and bring to a boil. Season with 2 tablespoons (30 ml) of fish sauce (or more, to taste) and the mushroom powder. Taste and adjust the flavoring with salt and pepper if desired. Add the noodles and cook for 3 to 4 minutes or until the noodles are tender. Alternatively, quickly blanch the noodles, then ladle into bowls and pour the hot soup over. Garnish with green onions. Serve immediately.

NOTES: For a shortcut, simply use fully cooked rotisserie chicken. Debone and pick out the meat.

If you cannot find or do not have mushroom powder, you may also add all-natural chicken bouillon cubes for extra flavor.

STREET FOOD FAVORITES

Visit any country in Southeast Asia and you'll be fascinated to see vendors, especially in big cities, on every street corner selling all kinds of food. We truly love to eat any time and all the time, which explains why there's so much food to buy everywhere. Hawker centers thrive and are the perfect places to try native delicacies as these are the areas where locals congregate to eat and where you're certain to enjoy delicious, authentic dishes.

In the meantime, and before your next trip to Southeast Asia, you can try making your own street food and favorite Asian snacks in the comfort of your home.

For a morning or midafternoon break, I love to have a slice or two of a deliciously tender and moist rice cake with the perfect crumb—called Bibingka (page 105)—with coffee. My father and I love to order Bibingka whenever we go to a mall in Manila as it never fails to please.

If threaded rice balls dipped in a luscious coconut caramel sauce appeal to you, then you'll have a blast enjoying Carioca (page 109) as I did when I had these for snack at recess during my elementary-school years. Another kind of rice ball treat is Pinaltok (Glutinous Rice Balls in Sweet Coconut Sauce, page 110). Glutinous rice is shaped into balls then cooked with ripe bananas, slices of jackfruit, shredded coconut and even with tapioca pearls. Your taste buds are treated to varying flavors and textures all smothered in a sweet and creamy coconut soup.

For an after-school snack, a bowl of Tutong (page 118) can't be beat! Roasted mung beans cooked with sticky rice in a creamy coconut sauce totally fills up the hungry tummies of both young and old alike.

Ampaw (page 121), puffed rice Filipino style, is sweet, crispy and deliciously addictive. The puffed rice is fun to make and you can cut these treats into squares or in any shape you want, so it's great to make them with kids.

For more delicious options, Serabi (Indonesian Coconut Pancakes, page 113) are always a great choice and so is Palitaw or Dila-Dila (page 117), soft and chewy glutinous rice cakes covered in coconut, sesame seeds and sugar!

For a more savory snack, you can't go wrong with stir-fried noodles like an easy, homestyle version of Mie Goreng (Indonesian Stir-Fried Noodles, page 106) or Pancit Habhab (Stir-Fried Egg Noodles with Pork and Vegetables, page 114) with some spiced vinegar as sauce on the side. Last but not least are Xoi Nhan Thit Chien (Fried Sticky Rice Fritters Stuffed with Pork, page 122), which are sure to please.

BIBINGKA
(Coconut Rice Cakes)

This rice cake is so tender, moist, delicious and with the perfect crumbs, you won't believe you're eating a cake that's actually completely gluten-free! It's so insanely good it can rival any regular wheat cake in taste and texture. Bibingka is often served warmed up with some butter on top and enjoyed with coffee either in the morning or mid-afternoon. It's delicious as a plain cake for everyday consumption, but for special occasions it's topped with extra cheese and some salted duck eggs, too.

SERVES 8

8 (7-inch [17.5-cm]) banana leaves (optional, see Note), softened

2 cups (230 g) rice flour, firmly packed

2 tbsp (28 g) baking powder

½ tsp salt

4 eggs, room temperature

1¼ cups (250 g) sugar

1 (13.5-oz [400-ml]) can coconut milk

2 tbsp (28 g) unsalted butter, melted

1 tsp vanilla extract

Prepare eight mini pie or tart pans by lining each with softened banana leaves that hang over the edge of the pans. The banana leaves are optional but the cake is traditionally baked in them because they add aroma and a subtle sweetness to the cake. If you cannot find banana leaves, line the pans with parchment paper instead. Preheat the oven to 375°F (190°C).

Sift together the rice flour, baking powder and salt. Set aside. Beat the eggs in a bowl. Add the sugar, coconut milk, melted butter and vanilla. Mix well.

Slowly add the flour mixture to the egg mixture, mixing the batter continuously as you do so. Whisk until the batter is completely smooth and has achieved a pourable consistency.

Divide the batter evenly between the eight prepared pans. Bake for 18 to 23 minutes or until a tester inserted in the middle of each cake comes out clean. Leave in the pans for 10 minutes then remove from the pans and transfer to a rack to cool completely. Serve warm or at room temperature with coffee.

NOTE: The Bibingka may also be baked in two pie pans or in muffin tins lined with banana leaves or parchment paper. Banana leaves can be purchased frozen from Asian stores. Defrost first, then clean the banana leaves by wiping them with moistened paper towels. To soften the banana leaves, simply run each leaf over a flame or over an electric stovetop. Heat until the leaves are deep green all over.

EASY MIE GORENG
(Indonesian Stir-Fried Noodles)

A delicious noodle dish need not be complicated, and this homestyle dish is anything but. Prawns or shrimp and vegetables stir-fried with noodles and flavored with sweet soy sauce make a simple yet satisfying dish. You may use chicken instead of prawns or make it fully vegetarian by omitting the meat or seafood. Add some chilis for a spicy kick!

SERVES 4

3 tbsp (45 ml) cooking oil of choice, divided

8 oz (225 g) prawns or shrimps, peeled and deveined

2 eggs

3 cloves garlic, sliced

1 cup (100 g) cabbage, roughly sliced

1 cup (125 g) choy sum or bok choy, cut into 2-inch (5-cm) pieces

1 (8-oz [225-g]) package cooked yellow egg noodles like thin wonton noodles, rinsed with cold water to refresh

3 tbsp (45 ml) kecap manis or sweet soy sauce

1 cup (60 g) bean sprouts

Salt and pepper, to taste

Fried shallots, for serving (see Note)

Heat 1½ tablespoons (23 ml) of the oil over medium-high heat in a wok or large skillet. Add the prawns or shrimp and fry for 3 to 4 minutes or until opaque and bright pink. Remove the prawns from the pan and set aside.

Adjust the heat to medium. Add the remaining oil. Fry the eggs and scramble briefly. Push the eggs to the side. Add the garlic and cook for about 30 seconds or just until aromatic. Add the cabbage and choy sum and mix with the eggs. Cook for 1 to 2 minutes or until the vegetables are just starting to wilt. Add the cooked egg noodles with the kecap manis and the cooked prawns, then mix thoroughly. Cook until the noodles are fully heated through. Add the bean sprouts and give everything a quick stir. Adjust the seasoning with a little salt and pepper to taste. Serve with fried shallots for garnish.

NOTE: You can fry your own shallots but bottled fried shallots may also be purchased in any Asian store.

CARIOCA
(Fried Sticky Rice Balls with Coconut Caramel Sauce)

Sweet memories are made of these! During my elementary-school years, these were my favorite merienda or after-school snack. They are so deliciously comforting—loaded with coconut flavor and smothered in a coconut caramel sauce. These crispy rice balls are so tasty that even my little boy, who doesn't like coconut at all, totally loves these!

SERVES 6 (24 BALLS)

2½ cups (315 g) sticky or glutinous rice flour

2½ cups (250 g) shredded sweetened coconut

1¼ cups (300 ml) coconut milk

2 cups (480 ml) cooking oil for deep-frying, or more as needed

1 (13.5-oz [400-ml]) can coconut cream

½ cup plus 3 tbsp (120 g) brown sugar

½ tsp salt

In a bowl, mix the sticky rice flour, sweetened shredded coconut and coconut milk until a dough forms. Scoop out about a tablespoon (15 g) of dough and shape into a ball. Repeat until all the dough is used up. A cookie dough scooper is helpful for this.

Heat the cooking oil in a saucepan over medium heat to about 350°F (175°C). To test if the oil is hot, dip a skewer into it. When bubbles form around the skewer, the oil is ready. Fry the dough balls in batches for 4 to 5 minutes or until lightly browned all over. Scoop onto a strainer lined with paper towels to remove any excess oil. Repeat until all the balls are cooked. Set aside.

In a saucepan, stir together the coconut cream, sugar and salt. Bring to a boil over medium heat. When it starts to boil, lower the heat slightly, stir and cook for 5 to 8 minutes or until the mixture has thickened.

Dip the balls into the sauce, or to avoid sticky fingers, thread about four balls onto a wooden skewer and pour the caramel sauce over. Serve individually or on skewers.

PINALTOK
(Glutinous Rice Balls in Sweet Coconut Sauce)

When I was growing up, this was my favorite weekend snack. Whenever I go back home, I still always ask for this because it is my childhood comfort food. Glutinous rice balls are cooked in sweetened and creamy coconut soup and may be accompanied with tapioca pearls and fruit.

SERVES 8 (70 TO 80 RICE BALLS)

2 cups + 8–9 tbsp (500–515 ml) water, divided

1 cup (125 g) sticky or glutinous rice flour

2 pandan leaves tied in a knot (optional)

1 (13.5-oz [400-ml]) can coconut milk

1 cup (165 g) cooked large sago or tapioca pearls

1 cup (165 g) frozen shredded young coconut, thawed

¾–1 cup (100–134 g) ripe jackfruit (fresh or bottled), sliced

1 cup (225 g) ripe cooking bananas like saba, plantain or burro bananas, sliced

½ cup (100 g) sugar

Slowly pour 8 or 9 tablespoons (120 or 135 ml) water into the sticky rice flour. Mix, then knead with your hands until it forms a pliable dough. Shape into small marble-size balls. These balls will expand as they cook, so make them no bigger than small marbles.

In a deep pot, bring the remaining water to a boil. Add the pandan leaves, if using. Drop the balls into the water and cook until they begin to float. Pour in the coconut milk and bring to a boil again. Add the cooked sago, shredded young coconut, sliced jackfruit, sliced bananas and sugar. Simmer for about 5 minutes.

Remove the pandan leaves. Ladle into bowls and serve immediately. This can also be served at room temperature or even cold.

NOTES: For a shorcut you can buy frozen sticky rice balls in Asian stores.

Use bottled jackfruit, preferably a Filipino brand, for a more tender and sweet-tasting jackfruit.

SERABI
(Indonesian Coconut Pancakes)

These tasty little pancakes are a favorite afternoon snack in Indonesia. They're traditionally made into mini-pancakes and cooked only on one side. The pancakes can be made plain white or jazzed up with natural food coloring from pandan juice for a brighter presentation.

SERVES 4 TO 6

1 cup (240 ml) coconut cream

½ cup (100 g) coconut sugar or dark brown sugar

½ tsp salt, divided

½ tsp pandan or vanilla extract (optional)

1 cup (125 g) rice flour

1 tbsp (15 g) white sugar

2 tsp (10 g) baking powder

1 egg, beaten

1 cup (240 ml) coconut milk

Cooking oil, as needed

To make the sauce, combine the coconut cream, sugar, ¼ teaspoon of salt and pandan in a saucepan. Stir to dissolve the sugar, then allow to boil over medium heat. Lower the heat, then simmer for 1 to 2 minutes or until slightly thickened. Transfer to a small bowl and set aside.

Whisk together the flour, sugar, baking powder and ¼ teaspoon of salt. Add the egg and the coconut milk. Stir to combine.

Heat a griddle or frying pan on low. Brush with a little oil. Pour about 1 tablespoon (15 ml) of batter for each pancake onto the griddle. Cook until bubbles form, then cover with a lid and cook for 1 to 2 minutes or until nicely browned underneath. Traditionally, this pancake is cooked only on one side so only the bottom turns brown. Repeat until the rest of the batter is used up.

Serve along with the sauce.

PANCIT HABHAB
(Stir-Fried Egg Noodles with Pork and Vegetables)

What makes this noodle dish unique is the way you eat it. Sold on the streets of the city of Lucban in the Philippines, it's served on a piece of banana leaf and eaten using your bare hands, drizzled with a spiced vinegar sauce that truly elevates this dish from ordinary to extraordinary!

SERVES 8 TO 10

1 lb (455 g) pork belly, thinly sliced

1 tsp salt

4 cloves garlic, chopped

2 shallots, chopped

1½ cups (165 g) carrots, julienned

1 chayote, sliced

2 cups (480 ml) water

2 cups (480 ml) reduced-sodium chicken stock or broth

3 tbsp (45 ml) soy sauce

2 tbsp (30 ml) oyster sauce

1½ tbsp (23 g) brown sugar

1 lb (455 g) dried pancit canton (egg/wheat noodles)

2 cups (105 g) bok choy, roughly chopped

Pepper, to taste

Spiced vinegar, for serving (see Note)

Season the pork belly with the salt.

Heat a wok or large skillet over medium-high heat. Add the sliced pork belly and cook until fully browned and crispy. The pork belly has enough fat that adding oil to the pan won't be necessary. Remove the pork from the pan and set aside. Drain the fat out of the wok except for about 1 tablespoon (15 ml). Adjust the heat to medium. Add the garlic and shallots and stir-fry for 1 minute. Add the carrots and chayote and stir-fry for 1 to 2 minutes or until the vegetables are tender-crisp.

Pour the water and chicken stock into the wok. Season with the soy sauce, oyster sauce and sugar. Bring to a boil then lower the heat and simmer for 2 minutes. Return half of the pork belly to the pan and add the noodles to the simmering broth. Stir well to ensure the noodles get soaked in the sauce. Cook until the noodles are tender and most of the liquid has been absorbed. Add the bok choy and cook just until it begins to wilt. Transfer to a plate or a banana leaf and garnish with the remaining pork belly. Serve with the spiced vinegar on the side. Drizzle a few drops of spiced vinegar as you eat the noodles.

NOTE: To make the spiced vinegar, add some red sliced chilis, garlic and freshly ground pepper (to taste) to sugar-cane vinegar or rice vinegar in a small condiment bowl. Sugar-cane vinegar from the Philippines can be found in Asian stores.

PALITAW OR DILA-DILA
(Flat Rice Cakes)

Whether the name of this dish is derived from the word "litaw," which means "to show up," as these flattened dough balls rise to the surface of the water when cooked, or from "dila-dila" because their shape resembles that of the tongue in Filipino, these tender and chewy sticky rice treats are delicious smothered in grated coconut and then sprinkled all over with sugar and sesame seeds! Now, who cares about the name?

SERVES 8 TO 10 (24 PIECES)

2 cups (250 g) sticky or glutinous rice flour

¾ cup + 1–2 tbsp (193–208 ml) water

1 cup (225 g) sugar

1 cup (120 g) sesame seeds, roasted

1 cup (75 g) grated or shredded coconut, steamed or rehydrated (see Note)

8 cups (2 L) water, or more as needed

Combine the sticky rice flour with ¾ cup plus 1 to 2 tablespoons (193 to 208 ml) water and mix until a pliable dough is formed. Knead a few times to form a mass. Scoop out about 1 rounded tablespoon (15 g) of dough. Using a cookie-dough scooper helps with this. Shape into a ball then flatten into an oval shape roughly 3 inches (7.5 cm) in length and about ¼ inch (1 cm) thin.

Mix the sugar and roasted sesame seeds and place on a platter. Place the shredded coconut on another plate. Set aside.

In a large saucepan, bring 8 cups (2 L) of water to a boil. The water should be deep enough to allow the dough to float. In batches, drop the flattened dough into the water and cook until the dough begins to float. Scoop out the cooked dough and roll it in the grated coconut and then in the sugar–sesame seed mixture. Serve immediately.

NOTE: You can rehydrate the coconut by steaming it for about 20 minutes over rapidly boiling water. Steam the shredded coconut before you begin cooking the dough.

TUTONG
(Roasted Mung Beans and Sticky Rice Porridge)

Tutong refers to the crusty bits of rice that are left at the bottom of a pot when rice is overcooked (nearly burnt!). The bits are deep brown in color and have a roasted aroma and flavor. Filipinos love to eat that crispy crust! Crushed roasted mung beans have a similar color and aroma to that of the burnt rice bits, and perhaps this is why this rice porridge is similarly named. In fact, it is the roasting of the beans that give this sweet sticky rice treat a unique twist in flavor. Perfect for snacking, great for breakfast or even as dessert!

SERVES 8 TO 10

1 cup (220 g) green mung beans

4 cups (1 L) water

1½ cups (300 g) sticky or glutinous white rice, rinsed well

2 (13.5-oz [400-ml]) cans coconut milk

½ tsp salt

1¼ cup (250 g) sugar, or to taste

Regular, evaporated or condensed milk (optional, for serving)

Place the mung beans in a shallow pan or wok. Heat the pan over medium heat and roast the mung beans, stirring constantly, for about 10 minutes or until the beans turn dark brown in color. Remove the pan from the heat, transfer the beans to a plate, and allow them to cool slightly. Then, place the roasted mung beans in a food processor or mortar and pestle and grind until the beans are coarsely ground.

Bring the water to a boil in a large pot. Add the mung beans, then simmer, covered, for 25 to 30 minutes or until the beans are tender. Add the rice, coconut milk and salt. Cook, stirring occasionally, to prevent the rice from sticking to the bottom, for another 25 to 30 minutes or until the rice is tender. Add the sugar and stir until the sugar is dissolved. Taste and adjust sweetness if needed. You can add more coconut milk or water if you like a thinner consistency. Ladle into bowls and serve immediately. Drizzle with milk if desired.

AMPAW

(Filipino-Style Puffed Rice)

You might think it's difficult to make puffed rice but it's actually not. It's quite fun to watch how the rice puffs immediately when the grains hit the hot oil! This is the perfect snack for those on a gluten-free diet, too.

SERVES 8

4 cups (540 g) day-old cooked, cold or room temperature white rice, such as jasmine

2 cups (480 ml) cooking oil of choice, or more as needed

1¾–2 cups (350–400 g) white or brown sugar

⅓ cup (80 ml) freshly squeezed lemon or lime juice

Place the cooked cold rice in a shallow pan, spreading it out thinly and evenly. Dry the rice under the sun for at least 6 hours or until the grains are hard and brittle. Alternatively, dry the rice in a preheated 200°F (95°C) oven. Cook the rice for 1½ to 2 hours or until the rice grains look translucent, dry and brittle. The rice should still be whitish in color and not brown.

Heat the oil in a pan over medium heat. To test if the oil is hot enough, drop a few grains of rice into the oil and if they puff immediately (as soon as they're added into the hot oil or 1 to 2 seconds later), then the oil is hot enough. Fry the rice in small batches and quickly scoop out the rice with a fine strainer as soon as the grains puff up and turn white. Place the puffed rice in a bowl lined with paper towels to remove excess oil. Cook until you use up all the grains.

To make the sugar syrup, heat the sugar and lemon juice over medium heat in a nonstick wok or large skillet. Stir to dissolve the sugar and simmer over low heat until the mixture is bubbly, slightly thickened and sticky. Add the puffed rice to the syrup and stir, ensuring that all the grains are coated with the sugar mixture. Transfer to a lightly greased 9-inch (23-cm) square pan and spread evenly. While the mixture is still warm, cut it into squares using a plastic knife. You can also form the mixture into balls or form any other shape using a cookie cutter. Grease your hands with a little oil for easier handling. Remove from the pan and store in an airtight container if not eating right away, otherwise the rice would harden.

NOTE: The sweetened puffed rice may also be used as cereal for a delicious breakfast. Simply form the rice into small clusters after cooking. Then, just add milk!

XOI NHAN THIT CHIEN
(Fried Sticky Rice Fritters Stuffed with Pork)

Sticky rice stuffed with a yummy pork filling, then deep-fried until lightly browned and crispy?! Enough said.

SERVES 10 (20 LARGE RICE BALLS)

2 tbsp (30 ml) cooking oil of choice, divided

8 oz (225 g) ground pork

3 cloves garlic, minced

1 tbsp (15 ml) fish sauce

½ tsp ground pepper

½ cup (55 g) carrots, minced

1 cup (100 g) mung beans, soaked overnight or for at least 3 hours, drained

1½ tsp (8 g) sugar

1 tsp salt

3 cups (600 g) cooked Sticky Rice (page 33)

2 cups (480 ml) cooking oil of choice, for deep-frying

Soy sauce, for serving

Ketchup, for serving

Heat 1 tablespooon (15 ml) of oil in a pan over medium heat and add the ground pork with the garlic and cook until the pork has changed its color. Season with the fish sauce and pepper and continue to stir-fry until the pork is fully browned and cooked. Add the carrots and cook for another 2 minutes. Taste and adjust the seasoning with a little more fish sauce, if desired. Drain to remove any excess oil and set aside.

Steam the soaked mung beans over rapidly boiling water for 35 to 45 minutes or until tender. Transfer to a plate. Season the mung beans with the sugar and 1 teaspoon of salt. Mash either by hand or in a food processor until the mung beans are finely ground. Add the mung beans and 1 tablespoon (15 ml) of oil into the steamed rice and mix everything by hand, evenly distributing the mung beans.

Measure about ¼ cup (40 g) of the rice and mung bean mixture and shape into about 20 balls. The balls don't need to be perfectly round. When all the balls are formed, grease your hands with a little oil. Take one ball at a time, and place it in the palm of your hands. Using your thumbs, flatten the balls and create a well or hollow portion in the center. Add about 1 rounded tablespoonful (15 g) of the pork mixture to the well in the middle and then bring the edges together to seal. Roll the balls into your hands until you obtain a nice round shape. Place each rounded ball on an oiled surface to prevent the balls from sticking.

Heat the 2 cups (480 ml) of oil in a saucepan to about 375°F (190°C) and fry the balls in batches just until they turn light brown. Remove the balls from the pan and drain on paper towels to remove excess oil. Serve warm on a platter with a bowl of soy sauce or ketchup.

NOTE: For a shortcut you can omit the mung beans and just use another cup (100 g) of rice.

BEST WAYS TO BEGIN THE DAY

Because breakfast is considered to be the most important meal, it's essential to begin the day with something delightfully filling and scrumptious! Thankfully, there's a lot to choose from in this chapter, so your daily fare won't be boring and the whole family will enjoy their first meal of the day.

If sweet breakfast is your choice, you'll love the tender and slightly chewy steamed mini rice cakes called Puto (page 128) made from rice flour and coconut milk. This is my personal favorite and I always have this when I go back to the Philippines. I dare you to eat only one!

There's also Khao Neow Dam Sang Kaya (Steamed Sticky Rice with Coconut Custard, page 136) from Thailand, which are sold on the streets of Bangkok in the mornings. Fancy some rice pudding for breakfast? Then the sweet–salty flavors of Bubur Sumsum (page 140), a thick and creamy coconut rice pudding from Indonesia, will surely please your palate.

What is breakfast without some chocolate? Champorado (Chocolate Rice Porridge, page 132) and Suman con Chocolate (Rice Cakes with Chocolate Sauce, page 127) will satisfy your chocolate cravings early in the morning! Binutong (page 143) is steamed sticky or glutinous rice cooked in banana leaves shaped into small pouches. This is a perennial breakfast favorite from the Bicol region of the Philippines and is always paired with a hot cup of cocoa or coffee.

Fried rice is always a tasty option and Nasi Goreng Jawa (page 135), a sweet and spicy version from Java, Indonesia is sure to become a favorite.

Flavored with hoisin sauce, soy sauce and sesame oil, Chee Cheong Fun (Rice Noodle Rolls, page 139) are always a yummy and fun option for breakfast!

The list is not complete without a delectable bowl of congee from Thailand called Jok Moo (Rice Porridge with Pork Meatballs, page 131). It is both filling and satisfying!

Stop settling for the usual cereal and cold milk for breakfast, and check out why these delicious treats are the best ways to begin the day.

SUMAN CON CHOCOLATE
(Steamed Glutinous Rice Cakes with Chocolate Sauce)

Suman is a tube-shaped rice cake made with glutinous rice cooked in coconut milk, wrapped in either palm, banana or bamboo leaves, then steamed. It is always a great choice for breakfast as it can be paired with a variety of options: plain sugar, coconut jam, with fruits and, of course, a big favorite—homemade chocolate sauce. This breakfast treat is almost always paired with coffee or hot chocolate.

SERVES 8 (16 RICE CAKES)

2 cups (400 g) sticky or glutinous white rice

1 (13.5-oz [400-ml]) can coconut cream plus enough water to make it to 2½ cups (600 ml)

½ cup (100 g) white sugar

1¼ tsp (8 g) salt, divided

16 (9-inch [27-cm]) softened banana leaves for wrapping

2 cups (480 ml) heavy or double cream

6 tbsp (42 g) cocoa powder

½ cup (100 g) brown sugar

NOTE: Brush a deep pot with a little oil if you are not using a nonstick pan. This will ensure the rice doesn't stick to the bottom of the pan as it cooks.

Soak the rice in water overnight or for at least 3 hours. Rinse the rice well. Drain. Place the rice and coconut cream diluted with water in a wok or deep pan. Bring the mixture to a boil. Adjust the heat to low and simmer, stirring occasionally, for 15 to 20 minutes or until the rice is tender and the liquid has nearly dried up. Add the sugar and 1 teaspoon of salt and continue to cook until the sugar is fully dissolved and the rice begins to pull away from the edges of the pan when stirred. Remove from the heat and allow the rice to cool.

Defrost the banana leaves, if frozen. Clean the banana leaves by wiping off the white residue with a damp cloth or paper towel. Pass each leaf through a flame or place it on the stovetop to heat it up until it turns dark green. This will help prevent the banana leaf from tearing as you roll it up.

Scoop about ¼ cup (45 g) of the rice near the edge of the banana leaves. Flatten it to elongate to about 5 inches (15 cm) in length. Roll until you reach the other end. Twist the edges then tie each end with a twine or a thin strip of banana leaf. Repeat until there's no more rice left.

Place the rice parcels in a steamer tray or basket. Steam the rice parcels over rapidly boiling water for 30 minutes. Make sure that the water doesn't touch the steamer basket.

To make the sauce, place the heavy cream, cocoa powder, brown sugar and ¼ teaspoon of salt in a saucepan over medium heat and stir to combine. Simmer for 5 to 8 minutes or until the sauce is thickened and coats the back of a spoon. Set aside.

When the rice parcels are done, peel the banana leaf cover from each cake then serve the rice cakes warm or at room temperature drizzled with the chocolate sauce. Suman may also be threaded in skewers and dipped in the sauce.

PUTO
(Steamed Mini Rice Cakes)

Steamed mini rice cakes are always a delicious option for breakfast in Southeast Asia. Rice flour flavored with coconut milk and sugar are mixed together then poured in molds and steamed to perfection creating light, sweet and tender little cakes that are totally scrumptious! You can't have just one!

SERVES 6 TO 8 (18 TO 20 PUTO)

Butter, for greasing

1½ cups (190 g) regular rice flour, firmly packed

1 cup (125 g) sticky or glutinous rice flour, firmly packed

1½ tbsp (23 g) baking powder

¼ tsp salt

1 cup (240 ml) water

1 egg, beaten

½ cup (100 g) sugar

¼ cup (60 ml) coconut cream

1 tsp vanilla extract

Melted butter, for serving

Fresh or dried desiccated or grated coconut, for serving

Brown sugar, for serving

Grease muffin tins with a little butter. If using silicone baking cups, you will not need to grease. Set aside.

Sift together the rice flour, sticky rice flour, baking powder and salt in a bowl. Pour the water into the flour mixture and mix well. Add the egg, sugar, coconut cream and vanilla and mix everything until smooth and no lumps appear. Fill the baking molds or cups about two-thirds full to leave enough room for the cakes to expand. Place the filled molds into a steamer tray or basket. Steam over rapidly boiling water for 15 to 18 minutes or until a tester inserted in the center comes out clean. Remove from the heat and transfer the cooked puto to a cooling rack.

Serve the rice cakes warm or at room temperature. Brush with some melted butter and sprinkle with some grated or shredded coconut and a little brown sugar before eating.

JOK MOO
(Rice Porridge with Pork Meatballs)

Rice porridge is the oatmeal of Southeast Asia. Creamy, tasty and comforting, each country in the region has their own version. Some add chicken or seafood, some are simply plain while others are made with pork as in this delicious Thai version. This is definitely a yummy way to carry you through the day!

SERVES 6

1 cup (200 g) jasmine rice, broken or long-grain, cooked

5 cups (1.2 L) chicken stock, divided

5 cups (1.2 L) water, divided

1 lb (455 g) ground pork

3 cloves garlic, minced

1½ tsp (3 g) freshly grated ginger

1 tbsp (15 ml) fish sauce

1 tbsp (15 ml) soy sauce

1 tsp sugar

½ tsp ground white pepper

Salt and pepper, to taste

Hard-boiled eggs, halved, for serving

Ginger, fresh or fried, julienned, for serving

Green onions, thinly sliced, for serving

Rinse the rice well. Drain. Place the rice in a deep soup pot. Add half of the stock and water (5 cups [1.2 L] in total) and bring to a boil. Adjust the heat to low, then simmer uncovered until most of the liquid has been absorbed. Stir once in a while so the rice doesn't stick to the bottom.

As the rice cooks, prepare the meatballs. In a bowl, mix the ground pork, garlic, ginger, fish sauce, soy sauce, sugar and white pepper. Shape into 1-inch (3-cm) balls. This will make about 26 meatballs.

Boil the remaining chicken stock and water (5 cups [1.2 L] in total) in another pan. Add the meatballs and cook for 10 to 12 minutes or until the meatballs are cooked and tender. Remove the meatballs and pour the stock into the pot with the rice. You may add the meatballs at this point or ladle them separately into bowls. Bring the rice to a simmer and cook to your desired consistency. It should be porridge-like. Taste and add some salt and pepper, if desired. Serve with hard-boiled eggs, fried or fresh ginger and garnish with some sliced green onions on top.

NOTE: To make meatballs of uniform size, I use a small cookie-dough scooper of about 1 tablespoon exclusively for making meatballs.

CHAMPORADO
(Chocolate Rice Porridge)

If you prefer a sweeter version of rice porridge, then Champorado is perfect for you! Not only is it sweet, it is flavored with chocolate—and who doesn't want a little bit of chocolate for breakfast?

SERVES 6

3 tableas (Filipino chocolate discs or tablets) or 3 tbsp (45 g) unsweetened cocoa powder

1 cup (200 g) sticky or glutinous white rice

3 cups (750 ml) water

½ cup (100 g) sugar, or to taste

Evaporated or condensed milk, for serving

If using tablea, dissolve the chocolate discs or tablets in 1 cup (240 ml) of hot water. Set aside.

Rinse the sticky rice until the water runs clear. Place the rice in a deep saucepan. Pour the water into the saucepan and bring to a boil. Lower the heat to a simmer and cook, stirring occasionally, for 20 to 25 minutes or until the rice is tender and cooked.

Stir in the dissolved tablea (or the cocoa powder if using instead) and the sugar and cook until the mixture is thick and creamy. Taste and adjust the sweetness if needed.

Ladle the champorado into bowls and serve drizzled all over with either evaporated milk. Enjoy immediately.

NOTES: Chocolate tableas, which make champorado so delightful, may be purchased online, at Filipino groceries or at some Asian stores that may carry Filipino products. If you cannot find it, you can replace with other chocolate discs or tablets.

For a creamier or more luscious version of champorado, replace half the water with coconut milk.

NASI GORENG JAWA
(Javanese-Style Spicy Fried Rice)

If you love fried rice with a spicy kick, then this delicious Nasi Goreng Jawa is for you. So simple and easy to make, this rice dish has hints of sweetness and some heat that will perfectly accompany all your favorite Asian viands!

SERVES 3 TO 4

1 red finger-length chili, or more to taste

1 red long chili or red Fresno pepper

3 shallots, chopped

4 cloves garlic, minced

1½ tsp (9 g) salt, divided

2 tbsp (30 ml) cooking oil of choice

4 cups (645 g) cooked cold long-grain rice like jasmine or basmati rice, grains separated by hand

1 tbsp (15 ml) sweet soy sauce (optional)

¼ cup (60 g) fried shallots (see Note)

1 small cucumber, sliced

2 plum tomatoes, sliced

Grind the chilis, shallots, garlic and ½ teaspoon of salt to a rough paste using either a food processor or a mortar and pestle.

Heat the oil over medium heat and fry the chili paste for about a minute or until very aromatic. Add the cooked rice and mix well with the chili paste. Cook until the rice is fully heated through. Season with 1 teaspoon of salt and the sweet soy sauce for a pop of color, if using. Garnish with the fried shallots.

Serve with slices of cucumber and tomatoes on the side.

NOTE: You can make your own fried shallots by simply frying chopped shallots in oil until golden brown and crispy; but for convenience, you can buy these already cooked and bottled in any Asian store.

KHAO NEOW DAM SANG KAYA
(Steamed Sticky Rice with Coconut Custard)

You can't go wrong with breakfast that calls for coconut custard to be included as part of the meal. That is exactly what this is! Steamed sticky rice is topped with coconut custard for a scrumptious breakfast that doubles as dessert! I am all for that!

SERVES 6

5 eggs, beaten

1 cup (200 g) palm sugar or light brown sugar

2 cups (480 ml) coconut cream, divided

1 tbsp (15 g) rice flour

½ tsp pandan extract or vanilla extract

½ tsp salt, divided

2 cups (400 g) sticky or glutinous white rice

⅓ cup (75 g) white sugar

Preheat the oven to 350°F (175°C).

Beat the eggs and palm sugar in a bowl with a whisk or an electric mixer. Mix well until the sugar is fully dissolved. Add 1 cup (240 ml) of the coconut cream, the rice flour, pandan extract and ¼ teaspoon salt. Mix again until well blended and smooth. Strain the liquid using a fine sieve or cloth over two custard molds or ramekins. Gently tap down the custard molds to remove the bubbles that may form on top. Cover with foil.

Place the molds in a baking pan and add enough hot water to the pan to reach halfway up the sides of the molds. Bake for about 30 minutes, or until a tester inserted comes out clean. Cool completely. Refrigerate until needed.

Alternatively, place the strained custard in two bowls, cover each with foil then steam the bowls over rapidly boiling water for 30 minutes or until a tester inserted comes out clean. The coconut custard can be made 1 to 2 days ahead.

Place the rice in a bowl and fill it up with enough water to completely cover the rice by about 2 inches (5 cm). Cover the bowl and soak the rice overnight or for at least 3 hours. Drain the rice, then wash until the water runs clear. Drain well, then place in a steamer basket lined with a cheesecloth. Steam the rice over rapidly boiling water for 30 minutes. Allow to cool.

To make the coconut sauce, heat 1 cup (240 ml) of coconut cream with the white sugar and ¼ teaspoon of salt in a saucepan over medium heat. Stir until the sugar has dissolved. Bring to a boil then simmer over low until the sauce has slightly thickened. Remove the sauce from the pan and cool before using.

To serve, scoop a portion of the sticky rice into either a bowl or over a banana leaf as it is traditionally served. Pour a little coconut cream over the rice, then place a slice of the custard on top.

CHEE CHEONG FUN
(Rice Noodle Rolls)

Whether you have this steamed fresh rice noodle dish for breakfast or for a snack, it is sure to delight your taste buds. Flavored with hoisin sauce, soy sauce and sesame oil, it's a hit every time!

SERVES 4 TO 5

4 tbsp (60 ml) hoisin sauce

1 tbsp (15 ml) light (regular) soy sauce

2 tbsp (30 ml) sweet soy sauce

2 tsp (10 ml) sesame oil

2 (12-oz [340-g]) packages fresh rice noodles

2 tbsp (30 g) roasted sesame seeds

Combine the hoisin sauce, soy sauce, sweet soy sauce and sesame oil. Set aside.

Slice the noodles into thin (about 1-inch [2.5-cm]) strips, if they aren't already. Line a steamer tray with a banana leaf or grease with a little oil. Place the noodle strips in the tray. Steam the noodles over rapidly boiling water for 5 minutes or until soft and heated through. Alternatively, place the noodles in a deep dish and pour hot water over them. Cover and soak for 5 minutes or until softened. Drain very well. Place the noodles in a serving bowl.

Divide the noodles into individual portions and drizzle sauce over each, then toss to combine. Sprinkle with the sesame seeds. Enjoy immediately.

NOTE: Blocks of rice noodles tend to harden in the fridge. If that happens, just microwave briefly so the noodle sheets are easier to handle before you trim them. Rice noodles already trimmed into strips are also available in Asian stores. Use these pre-cut strips if you can find them.

BUBUR SUMSUM
(Coconut Rice Pudding)

The sweet-salty flavors make this thick and creamy rice pudding so yummy. Bubur Sumsum is a delicious option for breakfast when you fancy something sweet and comforting.

SERVES 4

1 cup (200 g) dark brown sugar

½ cup (120 ml) water

2 pandan leaves, tied in a knot

2 (13.5-oz [400-ml]) cans coconut milk

1 cup (125 g) rice flour

¾ tsp salt

Fresh mango or bottled jackfruit, for serving (optional)

Crushed peanuts, for serving (optional)

Combine the sugar, water and pandan leaves in a saucepan and simmer for 15 minutes over medium-low heat until the sugar is dissolved and the liquid is syrupy in consistency. Set aside to cool.

Bring the coconut milk to a boil, then adjust the heat to the lowest setting. Add the flour and salt and cook, stirring often, for 10 to 15 minutes or until the mixture is thick and creamy. Ladle into bowls and serve with the sugar syrup on the side.

Enjoy with some mango or jackfruit on top, or sprinkle with some crushed peanuts for extra flavor and crunch.

BINUTONG
(Steamed Sticky Rice Parcels)

From the Bicol region in the Philippines comes Binutong, a perennial breakfast favorite that can be enjoyed either savory or sweet but is always paired with a hot cup of cocoa or coffee. Binutong consists of glutinous rice mixed with coconut milk steamed inside banana leaves shaped into pouches.

SERVES 7

2 cups (400 g) sticky or glutinous white rice, soaked in water overnight or for at least 3 hours

1 cup (240 ml) coconut milk

1 tsp aniseed

½ tsp salt

7 (10-inch [25-cm]) sheets of banana leaves

Brown sugar, for serving (optional)

Line a steamer tray with a cheesecloth or softened banana leaves if the holes are larger than the rice grains.

Rinse the soaked rice until the water runs clear. Mix the rice with the coconut milk, aniseed and salt. Place a sheet of banana leaf in a bowl. Measure about ½ cup (100 g) of rice and place it into the banana leaf. Pull the ends of the banana leaf together to form a pouch and tie with a string. Repeat until you use all the rice.

Place the pouches in the steamer tray. Steam over rapidly boiling water for 30 minutes or until the rice is fully cooked and tender. Before eating, sprinkle with a little bit of brown sugar to add some sweetness if desired.

TEASE MY TASTE BUDS (SALADS & NIBBLES)

If you're planning an Asian-themed party, these unique and delicious appetizers are guaranteed crowd-pleasers.

Noodle-covered meatballs called Moo Sarong (page 147) from Thailand are so unique and tasty, everyone will be talking about them! If you desire crispy and crunchy bites, fried dumplings (Banh Goi, page 155) from Vietnam are sure to be a hit. My picky kids love these and if they do, everyone else surely will!

An Asian appetizer tray wouldn't be complete without deliciously crunchy spring rolls. The Vietnamese version of spring rolls, Cha Gio (page 151), are filled with ground meat, mushrooms and noodles and then perfectly seasoned with oyster sauce and fish sauce. A sweet, salty, sour and spicy dipping sauce complements these crispy nibbles!

For a light and summery appetizer, Goi Cuon (Vietnamese Fresh Spring Rolls, page 159) loaded with shrimp, greens and herbs are truly perfect. The peanut sauce that goes with these spring rolls make these finger foods insanely good.

What's an appetizer table without some tasty salads to choose from? Pick from Yum Sen Goong Sapparot (Pineapple Noodle Salad with Prawns, page 156), Yum Woon Sen (Spicy Mung Bean Noodle Salad, page 148), or how about some Nasi Ulam (Rice Herb Salad, page 152)? They're all equally wholesome and delicious!

MOO SARONG

(Fried Pork Balls Wrapped in Noodles)

These Thai meatballs are not only great as party nibbles but also quite fun to make. Kids and adults will have fun wrapping noodles around the meatballs. Thread the meatballs with toothpicks to serve as an appetizer and pair with a sweet chili dip or even Sriracha for some spicy kick!

SERVES 8 TO 10 (20 BALLS)

4 cloves garlic, peeled and chopped

2 tbsp (30 g) fresh cilantro or coriander roots, chopped

½ tsp freshly ground black pepper

8 oz (225 g) ground pork or beef

2 dried wood ear mushrooms, rehydrated, tough parts removed then finely chopped (see Note)

¼ cup (35 g) water chestnuts, drained and chopped

1 egg, beaten

1 tsp salt

8 oz (225 g) fresh egg or wheat noodles (thin wonton noodles)

2 cups (480 ml) cooking oil of your choice, for frying

Sweet chili sauce, for serving

In a food processor or using a mortar and pestle, grind the garlic, cilantro and black pepper into a paste. Mix this with the ground pork, mushrooms, water chestnuts, egg and salt. Alternatively, you can mix all the ingredients for the meatballs in a food processor.

Using a rounded tablespoon shape the meat mixture into balls. Wrap each ball with the noodles, a few strands at a time, making sure that the entire meatball is fully covered.

In a saucepan, deep fry the meatballs in hot oil over medium heat for 4 to 5 minutes or until golden brown all over. Fry the meatballs in batches. Drain on paper towels to remove excess oil. Serve hot or at room temperature. Serve with sweet chili dip or Sriracha sauce on the side.

NOTE: To rehydrate the wood ear mushrooms, soak them in hot water for 15 to 20 minutes or until fully hydrated and soft. Rinse well, remove the tough stem, then coarsely chop.

YUM WOON SEN
(Spicy Mung Bean Noodle Salad)

This cold noodle salad hits all the right notes: spicy, sweet, sour, salty and so refreshingly good. It's easy to make so you can make this for lunch when you suddenly fancy a tasty Asian dish!

SERVES 4 TO 6

2 garlic cloves, peeled

1 finger-length red chili, seeded

3 cilantro or coriander roots, sliced thinly

3 tbsp (45 ml) fish sauce

4 tbsp (60 ml) lime juice

3 tbsp (45 g) palm sugar or light brown sugar

2 cups (480 ml) water, or more as needed

1 tsp salt

8 oz (225 g) ground pork

8 oz (225 g) prawns or shrimps, peeled and deveined

6 oz (165 g) dried glass noodles or mung bean threads

1 onion, sliced into wedges

2 stalks Chinese celery, sliced into 1-inch (2.5-cm) lengths

2 plum tomatoes, sliced

½ cup (75 g) roasted peanuts

2 stalks green onions, thinly sliced

1 small head of lettuce, torn, for serving (optional)

Fresh cilantro or coriander leaf, chopped, for serving

Red chili, sliced, for serving

Using a mortar and pestle, pound the garlic, chili and cilantro roots into a paste. Set aside.

Mix the fish sauce, lime juice and palm sugar well. Add the garlic paste and stir to combine. Set the dressing aside.

In a saucepan over high heat, bring the water, salt and ground pork to a boil. When the pork turns white and is fully cooked, add the prawns and cook for 2 to 3 more minutes or until the prawns turn opaque and orange. Drain, then set aside.

Cook the glass noodles in boiling water for 3 to 4 minutes or until the noodles are tender. Rinse with cold water then drain.

In a salad bowl, combine the dressing with the cooked noodles, ground pork and shrimp. Add the onion, celery and tomatoes and toss everything gently. Sprinkle with roasted peanuts and green onions.

Place the salad on a bed of lettuce if desired. Garnish with the coriander leaf and sliced chili.

CHA GIO
(Fried Spring Rolls)

These spring rolls are usually enjoyed with a Vietnamese noodle bowl, but they're so tasty and filling, they can certainly stand on their own as an appetizer or snack.

SERVES 10 TO 12 (28 LARGE ROLLS)

For the spring rolls

1 lb (455 g) ground pork

3 cloves garlic, minced

1 onion, finely chopped

4 dried wood ear mushrooms, rehydrated, tough parts removed, then finely chopped

½ cup (55 g) carrots, minced

2½ oz (70 g) glass noodles or mung bean noodles, soaked in water for 20–30 minutes or until soft, then trimmed into shorter lengths

1 egg, beaten

1 tbsp (15 ml) fish sauce

1 tbsp (15 ml) oyster sauce

1 tsp sugar

½ tsp salt

½ tsp ground pepper

28 (8 x 8–inch [20 x 20–cm]) thin spring roll wrapper or pastry sheets (see Note)

2 cups (480 ml) cooking oil, for deep frying

For the dipping sauce

2 tbsp (30 ml) fish sauce

2 tbsp (30 ml) freshly squeezed lime juice

2 tbsp (25 g) sugar

2 tbsp (30 ml) water

1 clove garlic, minced

1–2 finger length red chilis, thinly sliced

Mix together the ground pork, garlic, onion, mushrooms, carrots, noodles and egg. Add the fish sauce, oyster sauce, sugar, salt and pepper. Mix everything well, using your hands if necessary.

Place about 2 tablespoons (30 g) of the filling in one corner of a spring roll wrapper. Roll the corner with the filling (spreading it a little) toward the middle of the wrapper. Fold the sides inward to seal, then continue to roll until you have about 2 inches (5 cm) left of the wrapper. Using your finger, brush the edges with a little water, then seal completely. Make sure the seal is tight. Place the finished roll on a platter with the sealed side down. Repeat until you have used all the filling.

Heat the oil in a saucepan to about 350°F (175°C). To test if the oil is hot enough, dip a wooden skewer deep into the oil. When bubbles begin to form at the tip of the skewer, the oil is ready for frying. Fry the spring rolls in batches, avoiding overcrowding, for 4 to 5 minutes or until golden brown all over.

To make the sauce, mix the fish sauce, lime juice, sugar and water in a small bowl until the sugar is fully dissolved. Add the minced garlic and sliced chilis. Serve with the spring rolls.

NOTE: These spring rolls are traditionally wrapped in rice paper, but by using thin spring roll wrappers or pastry sheets, they will stay crispy much longer.

NASI ULAM
(Rice Herb Salad)

This healthy and delicious dish consists of cooked rice mixed with flaked fish, chopped herbs and roasted coconut. It is a tasty salad that you'll make over and over again!

SERVES 4

4 oz (105 g) white-flesh fish filet

½ tsp salt, plus more to taste

½ tsp pepper, plus more to taste

1 tbsp (15 ml) cooking oil of choice

2 tbsp (10 g) dried shrimp, rinsed, drained then finely chopped

1 cup (90 g) Chinese long beans or green beans, finely sliced diagonally

¼ cup (40 g) shredded coconut, toasted and pounded (see Note)

2 shallots, finely chopped

3 cups (375 g) cooked red or white rice (page 13)

1½ tsp (8 g) sugar

2 tbsp (30 ml) freshly squeezed lime juice

¼ cup (10 g) mint leaves, finely chopped (optional)

¼ cup (10 g) basil leaves, finely chopped (optional)

¼ cup (10 g) cilantro or coriander leaves, finely chopped (optional)

2 tbsp (10 g) kaffir lime leaves, finely chopped (optional)

Lime slices, for serving (optional)

Season the fish with salt and pepper. In a wok or skillet, heat the oil over medium heat and fry the fish 3 minutes on each side or until cooked through. Flake the fish using a fork, then set aside. In the same wok, cook the shrimp for 1 to 2 minutes or until fragrant.

Blanch the sliced green beans briefly in boiling water just until they change color. Drain well. Set aside.

Mix the fish, shrimp, beans, toasted coconut and shallots with the rice. Season with the sugar and extra salt and pepper to taste. Drizzle all over with the lime juice.

Toss the rice with any or all of the herbs. Garnish with any of the remaining herbs and some lime slices on the side. Serve immediately.

NOTE: To toast the coconut, place it in a small frying pan and then dry roast over low to medium heat until it turns brown. With a mortar and pestle, lightly pound the toasted coconut just until it becomes a little moist. Alternatively, pulse the roasted coconut in a food processor until it looks like sawdust.

BANH GOI
(Crispy Fried Dumplings)

My kids are huge fans of spring rolls so it wasn't a surprise that they totally enjoyed these crispy-licious fried dumplings from Vietnam. This recipe makes a lot so it's great to serve these dumplings as a party appetizer. They're perfect for snacking, too!

SERVES 10 TO 12 (42 DUMPLINGS)

For the dumplings

1 lb (455 g) ground pork

3 cloves garlic, minced

1 shallot, finely chopped

½ cup (55 g) grated carrots

5 wood ear mushrooms, rehydrated, tough parts removed, julienned then coarsely chopped (see Note)

3 oz (75 g) dried glass noodles or mung bean threads, soaked in very hot water for 3–5 minutes or until soft, rinsed then drained, trimmed to 3–4 inches (7.5–10 cm)

1 tbsp (15 ml) fish sauce

1 tsp sugar

1 tsp salt

½ tsp ground white pepper

1 (12-oz [340-g]) pack round wonton wrappers

2 cups (480 ml) oil of choice, for frying

For the dipping sauce

3 tbsp (45 ml) fish sauce

3 tbsp (45 ml) lime juice

3 tbsp (48 g) sugar

3 tbsp (45 ml) water

3 cloves garlic, minced

1 finger-length red chili, sliced

In a large bowl, mix together the ground pork, garlic, shallot, carrots, mushrooms, trimmed glass noodles, fish sauce, sugar, salt and pepper. Set aside for 10 minutes to allow the flavors to develop.

Place about a tablespoon (15 g) of filling in the middle of a wonton wrapper. Dab the edges with a little water, then fold up so the edges meet, and pinch the edges together. Crimp the edges using your hands or a fork to seal. You can also use a dumpling maker or dough press to make the dumplings. Repeat until all the filling and wrappers are used.

To make the dipping sauce, combine the fish sauce, lime juice, sugar and water. Mix well until the sugar is dissolved. Add the garlic and chili and stir to combine.

Heat the oil in a saucepan to about 350°F (175°C). The oil is hot enough when bubbles form when a skewer is dipped into it. Fry the dumplings until golden brown, about 4 to 5 minutes. Serve immediately with the dipping sauce on the side.

NOTE: To rehydrate the wood ear mushrooms, soak them in hot water for 15 to 20 minutes or until fully hydrated and soft. Rinse well and remove the tough stem then coarsely chop.

YUM SEN GOONG SAPPAROT
(Pineapple Noodle Salad with Prawns)

Fast, fresh and delicious, this Thai pineapple, prawn and noodle salad is perfect for busy days or nights.

SERVES 4

4 tbsp (60 ml) freshly squeezed lime juice

3 tbsp (45 ml) fish sauce

2 tbsp (25 g) sugar

3 cloves garlic, minced

8 oz (225 g) dried rice vermicelli

1 (13.5-oz [400-ml]) can coconut cream

8 oz (225 g) large prawns or shrimps, peeled and deveined

1 cup (200 g) pineapple chunks

2 stalks green onion, sliced thinly

½ cup (75 g) roasted peanuts, crushed

Mix the lime juice, fish sauce, sugar and garlic in a bowl. Set aside.

Cook the rice noodles in boiling water for 3 to 4 minutes or until soft. Strain then rinse with cold water. Drain well and set aside.

In a saucepan, bring the coconut cream to a boil over medium heat. Add the prawns and cook for 2 to 3 minutes or until they are opaque and bright pink. Drain well and set aside.

Divide the cooked noodles into four bowls. Top with the prawns and pineapple chunks. Drizzle with the dressing. Garnish with the sliced green onions and crushed peanuts. Serve immediately.

GOI CUON
(Fresh Spring Rolls)

These classic Vietnamese spring rolls not only present beautifully, they are fun to make and definitely delicious! I love assembling these rolls with my little girl—she loves to pile on the veggies, meat and shrimp and then roll the rice paper—all on her own. If my 10-year-old can make these spring rolls, surely anyone can and it's certainly a great way to bond over good food!

SERVES 8 (16 ROLLS)

1 tbsp (15 ml) cooking oil of choice

3 cloves garlic, minced

½ cup (120 ml) hoisin sauce

1 cup (240 ml) water

½ cup + 2 tbsp (112 g) peanut butter, plain or chunky

2 tbsp (25 g) sugar

2 tbsp (30 g) roasted peanuts, crushed

6 oz (170 g) dried rice vermicelli

1 small head green lettuce, chopped

1 lb (455 g) medium prawns or shrimps, cooked and peeled

1 oz (28 g) basil leaves

1 oz (28 g) cilantro leaves

1 oz (28 g) mint leaves

1 medium carrot, peeled and julienned

8 oz (225 g) pork belly or pork loin, boiled in salted water until cooked then thinly sliced

1 (8-inch [22-cm]) pack round rice paper sheets (banh trang), about 16 pieces

Heat the oil in a small saucepan over low heat. Add the minced garlic and cook until golden brown. Add the hoisin sauce, water, peanut butter and sugar. Stir well to combine. Bring to a simmer and cook for 5 to 8 more minutes or until slightly thickened. Taste and adjust the seasoning, if desired. Spoon the sauce into a bowl and garnish with the crushed peanuts.

Cook the rice noodles in boiling water for 3 to 4 minutes or just until tender. Rinse under cold water then drain well.

Place the rice noodles, lettuce, prawns, basil, cilantro, mint, carrot and pork on a platter or in small bowls at the table where you will assemble the spring rolls. Have a large wooden cutting board or big plate on hand for rolling. In a bowl or pan large enough to accommodate the rice paper, add room-temperature water.

To assemble the rolls, dip one sheet of rice paper into the water, submerging the paper entirely. Remove the rice paper immediately, shake off any excess water and lay it flat on the cutting board or platter. Place some chopped lettuce on the bottom edge of the rice paper and three prawns side by side above the lettuce. Leave about 2 inches (5 cm) on either side. Place a couple of leaves from any or all of the herbs, a few carrot slices and a small portion of the rice noodles on top of the lettuce. Place a long thin slice of the pork on top of the prawns.

Roll the bottom edge of the rice paper up over the fillings, then fold both sides into the middle. Roll again until you reach the top edge of the rice paper then place in a large platter, seam side down. Repeat until all the ingredients are all used up. Serve with the peanut sauce on the side.

SATISFY YOUR SWEET CRAVINGS

When I was doing research for this book, I was amazed to discover the many creative ways in which rice is used for dessert. What's even more fascinating is the fact that even though many of the desserts in the region share common ingredients, the resulting flavors are quite distinct. For example, Wajik (page 171), a traditional Indonesian dessert or sweet snack made with glutinous rice cooked in coconut milk and sugar at first glance looks like the Filipino Biko or Sinukmani. These desserts look similar yet have contrasting features because the cooking techniques are not the same and the overall flavors have subtle differences.

Do you think corn can't be used for dessert? The delicious Ginataang Mais (Rice Pudding with Corn, page 172) will prove you wrong.

A favorite childhood sweet treat from Malaysia and Singapore, Ondeh Ondeh (Sweet Potato and Rice Balls, page 175) has a sweet surprise in the middle that will make you come back for more.

With a luscious caramel topping, Bibingkang Kanin (Sticky Rice with Caramel Topping, page 164) is sure to please anyone. I've brought this to church a few times and it's always well received.

Sweetened sticky rice always pairs perfectly with your favorite tropical fruits, such as mango, pineapple and bananas. No wonder Khao Niaow Ma Muang (Sticky Rice with Mango, page 163) is not just a Thai favorite but is equally popular in the Philippines and Vietnam.

Exotic-looking and truly divine is rice pudding made with sticky black rice! Whether it's the classic Bubur Ketan Hitam (Black Glutinous Rice Porridge, page 167) from Indonesia or the Vietnamese version, Che Sua Chua Nep Cam (Yogurt with Black Glutinous Rice, page 176), you won't believe how deliciously good a black rice dessert can be.

Where there's rice, there'll be beans nearby, and that is the case with this thick and creamy rice dessert studded with black-eyed peas (Che Dau Trang, page 179) from Vietnam that is so easy to make and totally delish! Another dessert with beans, this time black beans, is the rolled sticky rice cake with banana filling from Thailand called Khao Tom Madt (page 168). One bite and you'll be hooked!

KHAO NIAOW MA MUANG
(Sticky Rice with Mango)

Steamed glutinous or sticky rice is soaked in flavored coconut milk and served with ripe and juicy mangoes with some extra coconut cream sauce on the side for drizzling. A very popular dessert in Thailand, Vietnam and the Philippines, you can take this dessert to an even higher plane by adding toasted sesame seeds and crushed nuts! I promise, this dessert is addictive!

SERVES 6 TO 8

2 cups (400 g) sticky or glutinous white rice, soaked in water overnight or for at least 3 hours (see Note)

1 cup (240 ml) coconut milk

⅔ cup (130 g) sugar, divided

½ tsp salt, divided

1 (13.5-oz [400-ml]) can coconut cream

¼ cup (40 g) sesame seeds, toasted, for serving (optional)

4 ripe yellow mangoes, sliced, for serving

Rinse the rice well until the water runs clear. Drain and place in a steamer basket lined with a cheesecloth or softened banana leaves if the holes in your steamer are bigger than the rice grains. Steam over rapidly boiling water for 30 minutes. The rice should be tender but still retain some chewiness.

As the rice cooks, in a saucepan over medium heat, mix the coconut milk, ⅓ cup (65 g) of sugar and ¼ teaspoon of salt until blended. Cook, stirring occasionally, over medium heat until the mixture comes to a boil. Turn off the heat and set aside.

In another saucepan, stir the coconut cream, ⅓ cup (65 g) of sugar and ¼ teaspoon of salt to combine, then cook over medium heat until it begins to boil. Lower the heat a little, then allow to boil softly for 1 minute. Remove from the heat and give it another quick stir. Set aside.

Place the steamed rice in a large bowl. Slowly pour in the coconut milk mixture, stirring the rice as you do to ensure that the rice is well coated and the liquid is fully absorbed. Do not be tempted to add all the coconut milk at once or the rice may become mushy. Just add enough coconut milk each time to moisten the rice. Spoon into individual bowls, sprinkle with toasted sesame seeds, if using, and serve with some freshly sliced ripe mangoes and the coconut cream on the side.

NOTE: Sticky rice is also known as sweet rice, although it's not sweet in flavor. It may be purchased at any Asian store. Soaking the rice overnight, or at least 3 hours, will help soften the rice and shorten the cooking time. To soak the rice, place the measured rice in a bowl or deep pan and fill it up with enough water to completely cover the rice by about 2 inches (5 cm). Cover the bowl and soak the rice for several hours (preferably overnight).

BIBINGKANG KANIN
(Sticky Rice with Caramel Topping)

With a luscious coconut caramel topping, this sweet sticky rice cooked in coconut milk is truly delicious. Making it may require a bit of elbow grease, but the recipe is easy and straightforward.

SERVES 10 TO 12

2 cups (400 g) sticky or glutinous white rice

2 (13.5-oz [400-ml]) cans coconut milk

1 cup (240 ml) water

1 cup (200 g) white sugar

1 tsp vanilla extract (optional)

1½ tsp (9 g) salt, divided

1 (13.5-oz [400-ml]) can coconut cream

¾ cup (150 g) dark coconut sugar or dark brown sugar

Soak the sticky rice in water for 1 to 2 hours. Rinse well until the water runs clear, then drain. Line a small winnowing basket (see Note) with softened banana leaves. Alternatively, grease a 9 x 13–inch (23 x 33–cm) pan or line with softened banana leaves.

In a wok or large, deep skillet, mix together the rice, coconut milk and water. Over medium heat, bring the mixture to a boil, stirring occasionally. When the rice mixture starts to boil, adjust the heat to low and continue cooking, stirring frequently, until the rice grains have softened and most of the liquid has been absorbed. Stir in the white sugar, vanilla (if using) and 1 teaspoon of salt. Increase the heat to medium and continue to cook the rice, stirring constantly. The rice is done when the mixture begins to pull away from the pan, is difficult to stir and forms one whole cohesive mass. Spoon the rice immediately into the prepared basket or baking dish, spreading it evenly.

To make the caramel sauce, stir together the coconut cream, coconut sugar and ½ teaspoon of salt in a saucepan and bring to a boil over medium heat, stirring constantly. Cook for 8 to 10 minutes or until bubbly and quite thick. Immediately pour over the cooked rice and spread evenly. Allow to cool completely before slicing.

NOTE: In the Philippines, Bibingkang Kanin is traditionally served in a winnowing basket, which is a flat, circular woven basket.

BUBUR KETAN HITAM
(Black Glutinous Rice Porridge)

The combination of sweet and salty is what makes this Indonesian dessert so deliciously good. This delightful dessert is usually served with a luscious coconut sauce, but a yummy alternative is a dollop of coconut ice cream on top.

SERVES 6 TO 8

2 cups (400 g) sticky or glutinous black rice, rinsed and soaked in water overnight

8 cups (2 L) water

2 pandan leaves, divided

1⅓ cups (235 g) brown sugar

¾ tsp salt, divided

1 (13.5-oz [400-ml]) can coconut milk

Rinse the rice well and drain. Boil the water then add the rice and 1 pandan leaf. Cook over medium heat for about 1 hour or until the grains are soft and the rice is thick. Add the sugar and ½ teaspoon of salt and continue cooking until the sugar has dissolved. Remove from the heat.

To make the sauce, place the coconut milk, remaining pandan leaf and ¼ teaspoon of salt in a saucepan. Cook over medium heat, stirring constantly, until it boils. Remove from the heat.

Serve the warm rice porridge with coconut sauce on the side.

NOTE: This dessert is perfectly made in a slow cooker, too. To make in a slow cooker, follow the instructions above but reduce the amount of water to 6 cups (1.5 L). Place the rinsed rice, pandan leaves and water in the slow cooker and cook on high for 3 to 4 hours or until the liquid is fully absorbed and the rice is tender and fully cooked. (Slow cooker temperatures vary, so adjust the cooking time accordingly.) When the rice is cooked, stir in the sugar and salt until the sugar is dissolved.

KHAO TOM MADT
(Thai Bananas in Steamed Sticky Rice)

What I love about this rice dessert is the pleasant surprise that you get when you bite into it. When I first tasted it on the streets of Bangkok, I thought it was just your usual plain rice cake studded with beans on top. I was so surprised when I bit into a sweet and fruity banana filling in the middle of these delectable steamed rice treats!

SERVES 10

2 cups (400 g) sticky or glutinous white rice

1 (13.5-oz [400-ml]) can coconut milk

½ cup (100 g) sugar

¾ tsp salt

10 pieces banana leaves or aluminum foil, cleaned and then trimmed to 8 x 10 inches (20 x 30 cm)

1 (15.5-oz [439-g]) can black beans, rinsed and drained well

5 ripe bananas, halved and sliced lengthwise

Soak the sticky rice in water overnight or for at least 3 hours. Rinse the rice until the water runs clear. Drain.

Brush a deep pan or wok with a little oil if not using a nonstick pan. This will help prevent the rice from sticking to the bottom. Mix together the sticky rice, coconut milk, sugar and salt in the wok or pan. Bring to a boil over medium heat then adjust the heat to low and cook, stirring often, until the rice has softened and the coconut milk has been fully absorbed, about 15 to 20 minutes. Continue to cook until the rice gets really sticky, hard to stir and begins to pull away from the edges of the pan, forming a mass. Remove from the heat. Allow the mixture to cool for 15 minutes.

In the meantime, soften the banana leaves by running them, one at a time, over a flame or on the stovetop until the leaf turns dark green.

Place about six black beans on top of each banana leaf. Make sure to use beans that don't have torn skin. Place 2 tablespoons (30 g) of sticky rice on top of the beans, then a piece of banana, more rice to cover the banana and finish with a few more beans on top. Roll up the leaves, fold in the sides and tuck underneath to seal.

Repeat until all the bananas and the rice are used up. Place the rolls in a steaming basket and steam for 30 minutes over rapidly boiling water. Transfer to a plate and allow to cool. Unwrap and serve warm or at room temperature.

WAJIK

(Glutinous Rice Cakes Cooked in Coconut Milk)

This sweet sticky rice dessert is made with rice that is steamed to soften the grains and then cooked with coconut milk and sugar until very thick and creamy. Such a tasty and filling dessert!

SERVES 8 TO 10

2 cups (400 g) sticky or glutinous white rice

2 pandan leaves, torn or cut up

1 (13.5-oz [400-ml]) can coconut milk

1 cup (200 g) palm sugar or brown sugar

½ tsp salt

½ tsp pandan extract (optional)

Banana leaf

Soak the rice in water overnight or for at least 3 hours. Rinse the rice until the water runs clear. Drain well. Place the rice in a steamer basket lined with a cheesecloth or softened banana leaves if the holes in your steamer are bigger than the rice grains. Add the pandan leaves. Steam the rice over rapidly boiling water for 30 minutes or until the rice is fully cooked and tender.

Transfer the rice to a bowl. Remove the pandan leaves.

In a saucepan, mix the coconut milk, sugar, salt and pandan extract, if using, over medium heat. Cook until the sugar has dissolved and the mixture is fully heated through but not boiling. Slowly pour the mixture over the rice, folding the rice gently to ensure everything is well coated. Cover and let rest for 30 minutes.

Place the rice in a wok. Heat over low heat and stir the mixture continuously until it gets really sticky and starts to pull away from the sides of the wok. This part requires a bit of patience and elbow grease. It's done when the rice mixture forms into a cohesive mass and it becomes difficult to stir.

Spoon the rice into an 8 x 8–inch (20 x 20–cm) dish lined with a banana leaf and spread evenly. Allow the rice to cool down slightly, then cut into diamond-shaped slices using a plastic knife for easier slicing. Serve warm or at room temperature.

GINATAANG MAIS
(Rice Pudding with Corn)

Sticky rice cooked in coconut milk with added corn kernels and cream-style corn make this one delightfully pleasing dessert. With readily available ingredients, making this dish is a breeze.

SERVES 6 TO 8

1 cup (200 g) sticky or glutinous white rice

1 tsp cooking oil of choice

3 (13.5-oz [400-ml]) cans coconut milk, divided

1 cup (200 g) sugar

1 tsp salt

1 tsp vanilla extract

1 (15-oz [425-g]) can whole-kernel corn, drained

1 (8-oz [225-g]) can cream-style corn

Rinse the rice well or until the water runs clear. Drain. Grease a large pot or pan all over with about 1 teaspoon of oil. This will help prevent the rice from sticking to the bottom of the pan as it cooks. In the greased pot, combine the sticky rice and 2 cans of coconut milk and bring to a boil, stirring frequently, over medium heat. Adjust the heat to the lowest setting then cover and continue to cook, stirring occasionally, for 15 to 20 minutes or until the rice is tender. Uncover and add the remaining can of coconut milk, sugar, salt, vanilla, the canned corn kernels and cream-style corn. Simmer for another 5 minutes until the mixture is creamy and thick. Taste and adjust the sweetness if desired. Spoon into dessert bowls and serve immediately.

ONDEH ONDEH
(Sweet Potato and Rice Balls)

These little rice balls cooked in boiling water, then rolled in shredded coconut are addictive. One bite and you'll see why! There's a hidden sweet surprise inside these little nibbles of deliciousness. Ondeh Ondeh are quite fun to make with the kids, too. This dish is a childhood favorite in Southeast Asia.

SERVES 8 (28 BALLS)

2–3 medium-sized purple or orange sweet potatoes, peeled and sliced

1 cup (125 g) sticky or glutinous rice flour

2–4 tbsp (30–60 ml) coconut milk or water

½ cup (100 g) shaved dark palm or coconut sugar (see Notes)

4 cups (1 L) water, or more as needed

1 cup (75 g) flaked or shredded coconut, steamed (see Notes)

Steam the sweet potatoes over rapidly boiling water for 10 to 15 minutes or until tender. Mash the cooked potatoes, then measure about 1½ cups (375 g). (You may have some left over.) Mix the mashed potatoes with the rice flour. Pour the coconut milk or water, 1 tablespoon (15 ml) at a time, into the potato and flour mixture and knead until a smooth, pliable dough forms.

Scoop out about 1 tablespoon (15 g) of the dough and shape it into a small ball, creating a well or hollow space in the center using both thumbs. Place about ¾ to 1 teaspoon of shaved palm sugar in the center. Fold the edges up over the sugar and reshape into a ball. Make sure that the sugar does not leak out on any side. Repeat until all the dough is used up. Set aside.

Fill a medium saucepan about halfway with the water. Bring the water to a boil over medium heat, then gently drop the balls into the water, working in batches. Cook for 3 minutes or until the balls begin to float to the surface. Scoop the floating rice balls out with a strainer and shake off the excess water, then roll in the flaked coconut.

Serve warm or at room temperature.

NOTES: Palm sugar in blocks is sold in Asian stores. Get the dark-colored palm sugar if it is available. Shave or grate the blocks for use in this recipe.

If using dried coconut, simply steam over rapidly boiling water for 15 minutes to rehydrate.

CHE SUA CHUA NEP CAM
(Yogurt with Black Glutinous Rice)

This refreshing dessert will surely cool you down on a hot summer day! The tart flavor of the yogurt contrasts so well with the sweet-salty flavor of the black rice pudding. Easy to make, this is a truly delicious and wholesome dessert.

SERVES 6

1 cup (200 g) sticky or glutinous black rice

4 cups (1 L) water

¾ cup (150 g) brown sugar

¼ tsp salt

1 (32-oz [907-g]) tub vanilla-flavored yogurt

Mint sprigs, for garnish

Soak the black sticky rice overnight or for at least 3 hours in enough water to cover the rice by at least 2 inches (5 cm).

Rinse the rice well. Bring the water to a boil in a saucepan over high heat, then add the rice. Reduce the heat to medium and cook the rice for 1 hour or until the grains are tender. Check the rice about halfway through the cooking time. When the rice is tender, add the sugar and salt, stir, then cook until sugar is dissolved and the porridge is thick.

Che Sua Chua Nep Cam can be served hot, warm, at room temperature or chilled. Serve in individual bowls or glasses topped with some yogurt and garnished with mint sprigs.

CHE DAU TRANG
(Rice Pudding with Black-Eyed Peas)

This is an example of a simple dessert that is creamy, sweet and truly delightful. It is also the perfect treat to cook in your rice cooker because everything is done for you—simply dump in the ingredients and walk away!

SERVES 6

1 cup (200 g) sticky or glutinous white rice

3 cups (720 ml) water

1 cup (240 ml) coconut cream

1 tsp pandan or vanilla extract

1 cup (200 g) sugar

½ tsp salt

1 (15-oz [425-g]) can black-eyed peas, rinsed very well then drained

Rinse the glutinous rice until the water runs clear. Drain well. Place the rice in a saucepan or rice cooker and add the water. Bring to a boil, then cover and simmer over low heat for 20 to 25 minutes or until the water has been fully absorbed. If using a rice cooker just push the "Cook" button to begin cooking and wait until it is done.

Add the coconut cream, pandan, sugar, salt and black-eyed peas. Stir gently until everything is combined. Simmer over low heat, stirring occasionally, until the mixture is thick and creamy. If using a rice cooker, push the "Cook" button again and wait until it shuts off and goes into warm mode. Taste and adjust the sweetness if desired. Serve hot, warm or cold.

QUICK GUIDE TO INGREDIENTS AND HELPFUL TOOLS FOR ASIAN COOKING

The authentic recipes from Southeast Asia in this cookbook may sometimes call for ingredients or tools that are not too familiar. However, Asian grocery stores now abound and even many big grocery stores have an Asian section. Here's a quick guide to these staples and where to find them. I also made some substitution suggestions if an ingredient is not readily available.

BANANA LEAVES Frozen banana leaves are available in the freezer section of any Asian grocery store. Simply thaw the leaves first, then wipe with a damp cloth or paper towel to clean and remove any white residue. To soften, pass the leaves over a flame or over a heated stovetop briefly or until the leaves turn dark green all over. Softening the leaves will prevent them from tearing. Banana leaves may be used to line a steamer tray or any dish before baking or cooking. They are often used to wrap rice or meat as well because the leaves impart a delicious aroma and subtle sweet flavor to the dish.

BELACAN This is dried shrimp paste from Malaysia and needs to be toasted before using to release its flavors. Only a little bit is used in most recipes because it's pretty potent.

CHILIS Finger-length or finger red chilis are medium-sized chilis about the size of a little finger, hence the name. They grow to about 1¾ to 2 inches (4 to 5 cm) in length and are commonly known as "Thai chilis." They can be found fresh, frozen or dried at Asian stores. These chilis are quite hot so just use enough to reach the level of spiciness you can tolerate. Mild red chilis about 6 inches (15 cm) in length may be substituted, but if these aren't available, red Fresno or Anaheim peppers are a good substitute. If using dried chilis, soak them first in hot water to rehydrate, then deseed and slice as required.

CHILI PASTE It's actually not difficult to make a basic chili paste from scratch. Simply hydrate some dried chilis in hot water, grind them to a paste with some garlic and shallots, then season with sugar and salt to taste. Dried shrimp or shrimp paste may be added, too. Otherwise, bottled sambal or chili sauces are available in Asian groceries.

COCONUT CREAM AND COCONUT MILK A lot of grocery stores now carry coconut cream or coconut milk in their Asian section, so these canned varieties are very easy to find. For best results, use a good quality coconut cream or coconut milk without preservatives or additives. It makes a huge difference in taste.

COCONUT MEAT Whether flaked, shredded, grated or desiccated coconut, meat may be found dried or frozen in grocery stores. If using dried coconut as a substitute for freshly-grated coconut, simply hydrate by soaking in hot water then drain before using or steam for 15 minutes to regain some moisture.

DRIED ANCHOVIES Known as "Ikan bilis" in Malaysia or simply "dilis" in the Philippines, these are tiny dried and salted fish sold in packages. Follow the package instructions on how to prepare them for cooking. Some may need cleaning or rinsing but others may be ready to use.

EBI/HIBE OR DRIED SHRIMP These are shrunken sun-dried shrimp that are salty, fishy and chewy in texture and add a lot of umami flavor to any Asian dish. Soak the shrimp first in hot water to rehydrate before using, unless a recipe states otherwise. Keep the soaking water for use in soups or stews as this has all the flavor from the shrimp and will enliven any dish. These are available in the frozen or refrigerated section of any Asian store.

FISH SAUCE This ingredient is a must for any Southeast Asian cooking. Most recipes call for this sauce as a seasoning. Make sure to purchase the highest or purest quality you can find with no additives, because this makes a difference in flavoring the dishes.

GALANGAL While this fragrant root looks somewhat similar to its relative, the ginger root, it doesn't taste the same. This aromatic rhizome has citrusy flavor undertones. Fortunately, galangal is now sold either fresh or frozen and even in powdered form in Asian stores. It may be sliced then sealed and kept in the freezer for weeks. Buy a big one when you find it, then slice into pieces and freeze. It will last a long time since you usually only need a few slices for cooking.

KAFFIR LIME LEAVES This very fragrant leaf is actually composed of two leaves attached to each other. These lime leaves are often added to curries, soups and stews to impart citrusy flavor and aroma to the dish. The leaves are usually torn, bruised or finely shredded before being added to the dish as the leaves can be tough to chew on. Fresh or frozen leaves are available at Asian grocery stores. To emulate the flavor of kaffir limes, you can add some fresh lime or lemon juice to the dish along with some bay leaves.

LEMONGRASS Fresh, frozen or even ready-to-use chopped lemongrass may now be found in Asian grocery stores. To use, remove the outer layer and use only the whitish thick bottom part of the stalk. Lemongrass adds an aromatic and lemony flavor to a dish but you may substitute citrus peel or lemon and lime zest.

MUSHROOMS Dried wood ear mushrooms (or black fungus) are easy to find at Asian grocery stores. These mushrooms, which look like big ears when dehydrated, are used not so much for flavoring but to add some meaty texture to a dish. These mushrooms absorb the flavor of the dish.

NOODLES Each country in Southeast Asia has their own names for, and types of, noodles and the recipes specifically mention which noodles to use to avoid any confusion. However, the commonality among these different noodles stem from what they are made from—either rice, wheat, eggs (yellowish in color and always contain wheat), or mung beans like glass noodles. Fresh, frozen and dried noodles are readily available in Asian stores. If using dried noodles, especially if made from rice, the noodles should be soaked or softened first in room-temperature (not hot) water as this is the best way to rehydrate them. The length of soaking time varies depending on the thickness of the noodles. For egg, wheat and mung bean threads, you can simply follow the package directions.

OYSTER SAUCE Oyster sauce livens up any food it is added to, like stir-fries or poultry, meat, fish and vegetable dishes. It is essentially made from oyster extracts, seasoned with salt and sugar and thickened with starch (and sometimes with added soy sauce for more depth of flavor). A gluten-free version of oyster sauce is now available for those on a wheat-free diet. There is also a vegetarian version called "mushroom" sauce.

PALM OR COCONUT SUGAR This is an unrefined sweetener made from a variety of palm trees that ranges from a light golden color to a deep dark brown. This sugar may be sold in solid form like round blocks that needs to be either shaved, softened or melted before using. Coconut sugar, which is a type of palm sugar, is now available in most regular grocery or health-food stores and may be used instead of palm sugar. Because palm sugar has a similar taste to regular brown sugar, the latter can be used as a substitute.

PANDAN LEAVES Known as screwpine leaves in English, these are available frozen in any Asian grocery store. Use one or two leaves to add a pleasant floral aroma to a dish. Pandan extract or vanilla extract may be used as a substitute.

RICE For regular white rice options, use either jasmine or basmati rice as they are easy to handle and cook. Broken jasmine rice, which is used for making congees or soup, is available at Asian grocery stores, but regular plain rice may be used instead. Glutinous rice is long-grain opaque rice, also known as sticky rice or sweet rice. Despite the name, the grains are completely gluten-free. When cooked, the grains tend to stick together and develop a gluey texture. Sticky rice is the base for many Asian desserts.

RICE COOKER While you can live without a rice cooker, it is very convenient to own one if you plan to cook rice often. It's so easy to use and all it requires is a touch of a button and voilà, perfectly cooked rice is on the way. No need to monitor the cooking as with the stovetop because it automatically turns off and switches to warm mode when the rice is done cooking. A rice cooker can be worth the investment and even many inexpensive rice cookers do a great job.

RICE FLOUR This flour is made from ground rice grains. There are two types of rice flour: one made from regular plain rice (rice flour) and one made from sweet, sticky or glutinous white rice (glutinous rice flour). Use the exact kind called for in the recipes in this book as they produce different textures when cooked or baked.

SOY SAUCES There are different varieties of soy sauce so it's important to use the particular kind called for in the recipe. There are light, dark and sweet soy sauces. Light soy sauce, despite its name, is not reduced sodium or "lite" soy sauce but is actually the saltier regular soy sauce used for dipping or seasoning. It's called light or thin to distinguish it from the thicker and darker variety. Dark soy sauce is less salty and is used primarily to add color and a smoky flavor to a dish. Sweet soy sauce, also known as kecap manis, has added sugar; it's darker in color, denser in consistency and is added to fried rice and noodle dishes for depth of flavor. All varieties of soy sauce are available at any Asian grocery store and in some regular grocery stores.

TAMARIND This fruit is very popular in Southeast Asian cooking, particularly in Thailand and the Philippines; it lends a fruity sourness to any dish. While tamarind is now available at many Asian grocery stores, for convenience, a concentrated form like a paste or sauce may be used instead. Tamarind paste or sauce in bottles may also be purchased online.

WOK If you enjoy cooking Asian dishes, it is worth it to invest in a high-quality, good-size wok. Both sweet and savory dishes may be cooked in it. A large and deep skillet is a good alternative to a wok. The nonstick variety is recommended for certain types of dishes.

ACKNOWLEDGMENTS

This book is a true labor of love. I don't mean my own work, but the labors of many friends and family members, who all contributed to making this book possible.

I first thank my family for all their support—my husband willingly drove me nearly every day to Asian grocery stores, even as far away as New York City, so I could get fresh ingredients for my recipes; my 10-year-old Sophie, my wonderful little sous chef, who chopped countless garlic cloves and shallots to help Mommy; and William, my just-turned-teenager, who became my designated dishwasher whenever I needed clean pots, plates and cutlery for cooking.

I next thank my dear sister Eunice Sotto and my BFF Ruby Cuevas, who generously devoted their time to join me in my travels to Southeast Asia. I appreciate that they both went on a rice and noodle diet with me! Thank you as well to the chefs and cooks from the region who generously taught me the best way to cook the most delicious rice and noodle dishes. I would like to particularly mention Lazat Cooking School (Malaysia), The Baking Loft (Singapore), Bangkok Thai Cooking Academy (Thailand), Ibu Dotty of Omahkoe Cooking Studio (Indonesia) and especially Chef Tan Viet Luong of Ho Chi Minh Cooking Class (Vietnam) for a very fun and memorable cooking class and most of all for teaching me how to make the best pho ever!

I also wish to thank my dear church friends who never got tired of tasting and testing the recipes I made for them on a weekly basis. A shout-out to dear Debbie LaFond for kindly painting and putting together the boards I used for my food photography.

Thank you so much as well to Will, Liz and Marissa for helping me make this project come true.

I thank the Lord Jesus for all His help in every step of the way. To God be the glory!

Abigail is the creator, photographer and recipe developer behind manilaspoon.com, a food blog featuring tried-and-tested, family-favorite home-style dishes from the Philippines, Asia and around the globe.

Abigail, originally from the Philippines, is married to Mark, from England, and they have two American children, William and Sophie. Her cooking reflects this multicultural background, and extensive travel around the world and in Southeast Asia allowed her to create meals that showcase delicious and authentic flavors from the many places she has visited.

Prior to becoming a full-time food blogger, Abigail was a law practitioner and was employed as court attorney with one of the justices of the Supreme Court of the Philippines, and later as a chief legislative officer for a member of the Philippine Senate. She pursued her master's of law at the University of Oxford in England.

Fifteen years ago, Mark and Abigail moved to the United States where Abigail rekindled her love and passion for cooking and thereafter started her own food blog (manilaspoon.com). She has created and photographed more than 500 recipes on this site. Some of her recipes have been featured in *National Geographic's Eating Healthy Recipe Guide* E-cookbook, *Taste of Home* magazine, the Huffington Post, Buzzfeed and Delish among others.

Abigail and her family currently reside in Hamden, Connecticut, where she continues to serve her family and friends her latest culinary creations.

INDEX